Minimalism for Families

D0963827

Minimalism
for Families

Practical Minimalist
Living Strategies to Simplify
Your Home and Life

Zoë Kim
Foreword by Denaye Barahona, PhD

ALTHEA
PRESS

To my husband, Sonny, and our children, Isabella, Maxon, Micah, and Marcus—without you I may not have seen minimalism. Thank you for growing me and helping me see what matters more.

And to every family making room for what matters in your home, in your mind, and in your heart—thank you, you're an inspiration to me. May your lives be rich in what matters most.

For general information on our other products and services or to obtain technical support, please contact our Customer Care Department within the U.S. at (866) 744-2665, or outside the U.S. at (510) 253-0500.

Althea Press publishes its books in a variety of electronic and print formats. Some content that appears in print may not be available in electronic books, and vice versa.

Cover photography © Petrenkod/iStock (boots); Pongsatorn Singnoy/Shutterstock.com (doormat); Sedat Seven/Shutterstock.com (wall). Author photograph © Raluca Rodila Photography.

Contents

Foreword

As a parent, I know firsthand that we want to give our children the world. Often that translates into giving our children more than we had ourselves. That means more love, more attention, more toys, and generally speaking...more stuff. This love and desire to provide for our children can be overwhelming—which is why *Minimalism for Families* is a vital read for all parents raising children in today's world.

Throughout my professional career I have studied families and researched how to raise well-adjusted children. As the founder of the online community *Simple Families*, I have worked for over a decade with families to find harmony and calm at home. I met Zoë Kim through our shared vision for improving the wellness of families. Both Zoë and I run online communities that serve families seeking both practical and philosophical support to move toward the solution for an overwhelming life: minimalism.

In *Minimalism for Families*, Zoë leaves no question unanswered. She believes that simplifying family life should be a quest for the family to take together, rather than children being led blindly by parents. As with all of Zoë's work, she is careful to include not only the *why* of minimalism, but also the *how*.

Making a life change, such as moving toward minimalism, is a huge adjustment. In this book, Zoë shows you how to turn off auto-pilot and live your life more meaningfully. You will start thinking more critically about making decisions and living with purpose and intention. This purpose and intention begins in our relationships and continues into our homes through the way we arrange our belongings and the choices we make about bringing new stuff into our living spaces.

Minimalism for Families holds your hand and walks you through every room in your home. This step-by-step approach provides the practical guidance and emotional support that you need to finally shed the stuff that is no longer serving you and your family. Whether your clutter is building up in your home office or exploding from your master bedroom closet, Zoë makes sure that you are armed and prepared to move these spaces toward minimalism and simplicity.

This book is a must read for all families. We must resist the temptation to overflow our families' lives with more stuff. This book guides us to teach our children to reallocate their time and energy away from material possessions and move toward a more meaningful, calmer, and balanced existence. This journey must start with us as parents. It starts here.

Denaye Barahona, PhD
New York, 2017

Introduction

There is joy in owning less. A minimalist life holds benefits for everyone—especially for those of us with families. Giving up excess stuff creates *more* time, space, and energy to pursue our purpose, passion, and meaningful connections with those we love. Will we ever look back and wish we hadn't spent so much quality time with those we love instead of the material objects in our lives? I know I won't.

Today's typical family has a life packed full of expectations and obligations. Our society pours out a never-ending stream of invitations to have more, do more, and be more. Not answering these invitations can feel like swimming against the current. But I often wonder, what are we swimming upstream for?

When your time and energy are divided among a combination of work, children, and a social life, charting a minimalist course for your family may look like one more thing on your to-do list that just isn't going to get done. Nowadays, it does take some work to simplify your life. So how can you and your family clear the clutter and stop swimming upstream? Start by accepting this invitation to help you and your family discover that *less* really is *more*. When our possessions and activities don't add up to happiness in our lives, it may be time to start subtracting.

My husband and I have four children. We know how quickly life can become busy and full of stuff. It seems every week there is an influx of things we are saying no to and things we are teaching our children to say no to as well.

Our journey to tackle our excess started seven years ago. We were a young family with two children under five. My husband was in the military and often deployed for extended periods of time. I was grateful and happy to be able to stay home with our children, but somehow I ended up spending more time doing things with our stuff than I did doing things with our children. I was exhausted and stressed, busy taking care of all our stuff.

With my husband halfway across the world on a surprise deployment, the kids and I had to pack up and move once again, this time from a rental home into a home we had purchased. Despite the fact that this was our third move in six years, we were moving just down the street. How hard could that be?

Well, the process of packing, unpacking, and organizing all of our stuff drained the joy right out of me—for an entire two months. It was during that stress, exhaustion, and desire to live better that I had an aha moment. I began to see the real cost of our stuff—and it was way overpriced! Thus began my journey to living a minimalist life.

Since we began de-owning our excess stuff and applying minimalism to other areas of our life, it's gotten easier to decline the daily invitations to *more*. Better still—it's easier to see and enjoy the freedom of *less*. I started writing about and recording my journey on my website, TheMinimalistPlate.com, to share with others and track my own progress.

Many people think they could never be minimalist with kids. Minimalism and kids under the same roof: How does that work? As it turns out, any family really can live a minimalist lifestyle. It works because it is practical.

In *Minimalism for Families*, I share tools, strategies, and concrete steps to help you integrate minimalism into your life and the lives of those who share your home. I give specific tips to de-clutter your home, sway your family to minimalism, shift your mindset, set down the heavy sentimental items, and tackle resistance. Through new perspectives, lessons learned, and actionable tips, your family can reclaim the values you hold so dear.

It's entirely possible for families to find their lives under everything they own. And this book is going to show you how. It will be different for each of us, but all of us will discover that there's more life in owning less.

Part One

The Minimalist Mindset

Minimalism appeals to a desire for a simpler life—an uncluttered and unbusy life filled with more meaning, purpose, and joy. This is a healthy desire, and pursuing it can lead to many benefits. Who doesn't want clarity of mind, financial freedom, contentment, a happy home, and better health, just to name a few? Chapter 1 is an introduction to the *why* of minimalism, what minimalism is, and what its benefits are. In Chapter 2, I will share the how-to steps I've learned to become a minimalist family.

1 The *Why* of Minimalism

It's important to know why you want to pursue minimalism. Having a firm grip on your *why* for becoming minimalist will be a steady source of fuel for your motivation to be one. This matters as much for those who are just beginning this pursuit as for those who have been after this for a while. And as you experience a minimalist life, you'll likely find new reasons to be minimalist. First, I want to tell you what I mean by *minimalism*.

What Exactly is Minimalism?

Since becoming a blogger and sharing our journey with the world, I've found a few questions come up often in the comments on my Facebook page, in person, and in my e-mail inbox. One of them is: What is minimalism?

My short answer usually goes like this: "Minimalism is about trading all of my clutter for the things I want more of: sleep, experiences, time with friends and family, and other things." If blog readers are still following along with me, I go on to tell them what minimalism is not—because these misconceptions are often what stops a person from a further pursuit of minimalism.

Minimalism is not about living in a tiny home and never owning more than 100 things (though you can certainly do that). To live as a minimalist does not mean you have to give up modern conveniences. There is one guiding principle for deciding what stays and what goes: figure out what brings value and purpose to your life, and let go of the rest.

Applying this principle is not a one-size-fits-all approach. Each of us—individuals, couples, and families—will use this principle for our particular season and situation. We will have different answers to the question of what brings value and purpose. You are reading this book because of your interest in minimalism. You also probably suspect that our culture's intense pursuit of having more and doing more doesn't lead to lasting happiness. Like me, you want to set about discovering how less really means more in your life.

Minimalism is a tool, philosophy, or filter to help you shed the excess stuff and live your life with purpose.

The philosophy of minimalism can be applied to any part of your life: what you own, what you do for work, what you put on your calendar, and how you relate to and connect with other people.

Minimalism helps you reassess your priorities so that you can identify and strip away the excess that doesn't line up with what you really want. Although the journey often starts with removing physical clutter, it also leads you to let go of the clutter from your heart and soul. It brings awareness to the void in your life that you're trying to fill with things that will not fill it, at least not for very long.

MINIMALISM IS A TRADE

When I think about minimalism, I don't think about what I must give up. It's not about setting a limit to the number of things I can keep. Instead, it's about what I'm trading. Giving up something is always about trading.

When we shed our excess possessions, we're making room for something better. *Everything has a cost.* When we say yes to one thing we are saying no to another. A minimalist life is about trading a life filled with clutter, busyness, and noise for a life filled with meaning, connection, and purpose.

MINIMALISM IS LIVING WITH INTENTION

When you apply the philosophy of minimalism to every part of your life, you practice intentionality. You ask yourself questions like: Do I really need this? Will this bring me joy? Does this grow my character? When we approach our day with the intention of discovering what brings joy and contentment, every subsequent action is filtered through this lens of conscious purpose.

MINIMALISM IS AWARENESS

As you apply minimalism and intentionality to your life, you start noticing how the predominant messages of our culture have influenced your past and present decisions.

You may be questioning the value of what you've filled your home with, the work you've chosen, and even the way you connect with other people. Are you spending everything you have in time, energy, and money on possessions, work, and relationships but still longing for more? Go back to less to find more of what you're really after.

MINIMALISM IS FREEDOM

Like it or not, we humans tend to make things more complicated than they need to be. We compare our lives to those around us and start thinking we should have what they have, do what they do, and be more like them. Minimalism helps you break free from keeping up with anyone else around you. It helps you discover what matters more for you and your family. It shifts your focus from what everyone else has, does, or is, to what satisfies you. We are free to focus on what matters when we're less distracted by all the noise and clutter around us.

MINIMALISM IS PERFECT FOR FAMILIES

The world today is a complicated place filled with noise and clutter at every turn. Minimalism is a philosophy that can help your family see and live the values you want to pursue and convey. Minimalism is a tool to bring balance into the lives of our families.

I like how Joshua Becker defines minimalism as "the intentional promotion of the things we most value and the removal of everything that distracts us from it." And Joshua Fields Millburn and Ryan Nicodemus (also known as The Minimalists) sum it up in one tidy digestible sentence: "Minimalism is a tool to rid yourself of life's excess in favor of focusing on what's important—so you can find happiness, fulfillment, and freedom."

So how might we apply this? The purpose of minimalism isn't really about the *what*, it's about the *why*. And as my friend Lisa Avellàn at the website *Simple & Soul* says, "It's not about the stuff—it's about your soul." I couldn't agree more!

In raising our children as minimalists, we are giving them the tools and filters to cut out the distractions and focus on what is really important. Minimalism gives your family the right kind of less: removing the distractions to focus on what's important and fulfilling—like one another.

The Soaring Cost of Excess Stuff

I invite you to think about your stuff for a minute. Think about the things that you own but don't actually use and may not even like now. Ask yourself if there are some things that you've forgotten that you own. How much time have you spent acquiring and taking care of things? As Henry David Thoreau said, "The price of anything is the amount of life you exchange for it."

Everything has a cost: your perfectly good things, your sentimental things, your useful things, the things you've forgotten you own. This doesn't mean you should discard everything and live in an empty box, but it does raise important questions, like why are we keeping so many things that don't bring lasting value and purpose to our lives? And why are we doing so many things that disengage us from what really brings us meaning and happiness?

We spend a lot of time on our personal belongings. We store them, clean them, find them, repair them, wonder if they're worth repairing, replace them, wonder what model to replace them with, consider what accessories to get with them, and search for the best deal for them. As you can see, personal belongings not only take up physical space but mental energy as well.

Let's face the reality that our deeper, heartfelt desires and goals aren't satisfied by more material goods and a really busy calendar. We're probably looking at diminishing returns in this crazy pursuit of *more*—spending our limited resources of time, energy, and money on homes overflowing with stuff and schedules overflowing with commitments, only to be left wanting more. Our overflowing calendars magnify the cost of our beloved stuff. The busier we are, the less time we have to take care of all of it.

There are tangible costs of our stuff, like money and space, but the greater costs are psychological. In today's culture, material goods have become substitutes for deep and meaningful connections. We strive to acquire possessions and busy calendars, and then ignore the things that give us lasting fulfillment and joy: personal growth, contributing to others, generosity, and healthy relationships.

The true cost of our excess stuff and chaotic lives reaches far beyond a price tag and a full calendar. Our excessive consumption is killing us and the people we want to be. I encourage you to never underestimate the benefits of removing things you do not need.

The Benefits of Minimalism

The less we have on our plate, physically and mentally, the more energy and gratitude we can have for the life we want and the life we have! When people think about the benefits of minimalism, they often think only about the initial benefit, such as an uncluttered home. But there are life-changing benefits to gain as you move past the initial purging. It isn't just a simple, clean home we're after. We're trading our excess stuff for things we'll look back on and wish we had more of, like time spent pursuing our passions and purpose and in relationships that bring positive transformation.

Minimalism directs your finite resources of attention, time, energy, and money toward being and doing more of what matters most. With this foundational benefit, you are better able to make the intentional choice to be and do who you're made to be and what you're made to do. This benefit is not just for some individuals who have the freedom to make drastic changes in their lives. All of us—including you and your family—will gain from it.

LESS STRESS AND ANXIETY

Less clutter equals less stress and anxiety. When we keep our environment cluttered, we are visually and emotionally distracted, and this creates stress and anxiety. In a study done by UCLA's Center on Everyday Lives and Families (CELF), a team of professional archaeologists, anthropologists, and other social scientists systematically observed and recorded details of life at home for 32 dual-worker, middle-class Los Angeles families between 2001 and 2004. The team discovered that managing a large volume of possessions was linked to elevated levels of stress hormones for mothers. They found that women in the study associated a tidy home with a happy and successful family. In other words, the more clutter that piles up, the more anxious women feel.

Our excess stuff is most likely affecting the stress levels of our children. The excess visual stimuli are a distraction for them as well. Less to take care of means less to stress about, and this can help us find more clarity of mind. Once the initial dopamine rush of getting something is gone, clutter becomes a relentless brain drain. Using MRIs and other diagnostic tools, research has found that clutter has a negative effect on our brain's ability to concentrate and process information.

Finding more clarity of mind is possible as we clear away the distractions that come with keeping more than we need and trying to be someone we aren't made to be. Just making a start on this path can give your mind more bandwidth with which to focus on what matters most in your life.

MORE JOY IN PARENTING

There is nothing like not sleeping well for months to make you feel unwell. Maybe it's just me, but very few things in life have tested my emotional stamina like becoming a parent.

Parenting is an enriching experience that is mentally exhausting. Many of us strive for the impossible ideal of the "perfect parent." We hold ourselves to unrealistic expectations. Being responsible for less stuff and fewer activities has helped me see the unrealistic expectations I was holding on to—and how they were affecting my mental health.

Finding joy in parenting becomes really difficult as we take on too much, own too much, and overfill our calendars for our family every single day of the week. Being mindful to not engage in busyness and accumulation makes it possible to entertain the meaningful requests of our children. Would you ever look back and say, "I wish I hadn't spent so much time with my family?"

STRONGER RELATIONSHIPS

Humans need to connect with other humans—we don't want to be lonely.

A minimalist home and lifestyle helps us put our focus on people, instead of on the stuff they have. There is more energy and space for people and relationships to flourish.

We don't build satisfying connections around possessions—not even shared possessions. Connections are built around shared experiences. I'm not saying that possessions have nothing to do with our relationships. But when we use a lot of our finite time and energy on possessions, we're spending time connecting to our stuff and our schedules more than we are connecting to other people. Minimalism is making a conscious choice to use things and love people, because the opposite will not bring us the connections we really long for.

HEALTHY BOUNDARIES

Minimalism helps you set healthy boundaries by giving you the clarity to see all the things you're spinning your wheels on. Resetting boundaries to align with priorities is an ongoing process in a minimalist lifestyle, but it's not an unwelcome chore. The rewards of more being and less striving encourage me to keep going on this journey. If I don't prioritize my life, someone or something else will.

MORE TIME

Keeping more than we need, whether it's possessions or activities, brings a fog into our daily lives that makes it harder to think clearly. Under the influence of clutter, we may underestimate how much time we're giving to the less important stuff. When we say, "If I could find the time..." we're really talking about how we choose to use our time. Minimalism helps you see how you're spending your time and to think more clearly about how you would really like to spend it.

We've found gap time in our family since we began practicing minimalism. This means we aren't living in the land of rushing around between one activity and another. Minimalism has helped us identify the activities, even the perfectly good activities, that take us away from better things. We no longer feel the pull to participate in every sport and enrichment activity that could possibly benefit our children. Remember, this is a good thing.

LESS STRESS ABOUT FINANCES

A minimalist approach to money management will free up valuable resources of time and energy as well as money. When we disengage from comparing ourselves to others and keeping up with our neighbors, we free up time and money. When we build our financial life on consuming, we're bound for discontent. Turn off or tune out advertising that encourages you to buy what you don't need. Less to take care of means less stress and more time to devote to other things. In addition, minimalism is a path to getting out of debt. There's no need to spend money on things to impress the people around you.

Financial minimalism has given us freedom to share with those who benefit far more from our excess than we ever will. But we aren't just giving away money or things that we don't need as much as others do. We're giving up money and possessions that we simply don't need. Not only do we not need it, this excess is at the very least a distraction, and at worst costs us more to keep than to give away!

A STREAMLINED HOME

Imagine having a home filled with no more than what adds value to your life. When you de-clutter, you're more likely to know what you have in your home. Finding what you need when you need it becomes an easier task when you develop clutter-free habits. Less frustration means less stress. Like a lot of other people, I strive to live in a clean and uncluttered home, but don't want to spend all my free time cleaning it. Having less stuff covering our floors, furniture, and kitchen counters has cut my cleaning time in half. Less time cleaning is more time to do something we enjoy more.

ENVIRONMENTALLY FRIENDLY

We waste less when we buy less and this is good for our planet. For the average American, clothing is cheap and readily available. One result of this is that the average American now generates 82 pounds of textile waste each year. Although I love a deal as much as anyone else, I no longer take pleasure in needless clothing purchases at my local Target.

Minimalism has helped our family take steps toward a zero-waste lifestyle. Just because we still need a weekly garbage pickup doesn't mean we can't or shouldn't keep taking steps to reduce our waste production. When possible, we choose products that can be used for a lifetime. For example, we discarded our plastic water bottles in favor of stainless steel ones. Since we each have and use our own water bottle, we keep plastic out of landfills and have fewer dishes to wash every day. Environmental minimalism helps you cultivate earth-friendly decisions, like choosing sustainable and recyclable beauty products, canceling your catalog subscriptions, choosing electronic media for books, magazines, and newspapers, switching to online banking and digital record keeping, carpooling or using mass transit, and limiting your shower time.

A minimalist home produces less waste, which is good for our planet and all of us living on it.

DEEPER SPIRITUAL LIFE

Many of us make a journey of faith to discover what we truly need and who we are meant to be. A spiritual journey can be interrupted by having too much and by having too little. Minimalism nurtures growth and discovery of who we are meant to be. Busyness is likely to give us a false sense of purpose and materialism is likely to give us a false sense of being blessed. We might not call it materialism when we post our pictures and stories with the hashtag #blessed on Facebook, Twitter, or Instagram—we probably want to express our gratitude and highlight our moments of happiness. But we can express our gratitude and contentment by giving what we don't need to someone who does need it. We can pursue and share our true purpose when we say no to commitments that don't serve it.

FREEDOM

Ultimately, minimalism gives you freedom. Freedom from consumerism, debt, and anxiety about caring for your possessions. Freedom from the weight of sentimental items. Freedom from guilt to keep things that no longer serve your purpose. Freedom from holding on to your fantasy-self and from measuring up to unrealistic expectations. Freedom to relax and think about what you want to think about. Freedom to say no to unnecessary obligations and to make better connections with family, friends, and neighbors. This is what minimalism is truly about.

Lessons Learned

Minimalism brings clarity and intentionality to the way we live our lives. Wonderful things happen as we loosen our grip on our stuff and our busyness—and get free of their grip on us.

WE ASK BETTER QUESTIONS TO MAKE BETTER DECISIONS

Minimalism has taught us to ask why before we buy. Our kids have caught on to this pretty quickly. They've asked questions like, "Will I want this toy next month?," "Do I need this?," "Would I spend my own money on this?," and "Is this going to make me happy?" We no longer buy something just because we see it at the store, a friend has one, or we can and it feels good. We buy things because we need them or because we believe they serve an important purpose in our lives.

LIVING WITHIN OUR MEANS BRINGS FREEDOM

Thankfully, our family is debt-free, and we want to keep that freedom! We show our children that living within our means gives us a contentment that can't be bought anywhere.

GIVING IS PART OF LIVING

Minimalism has taught our family that giving is far better than holding on to things we don't need. If you have more than enough, why not give some away? Our children have seen us invest more resources and donate more things to others since embracing a minimalist lifestyle. As a result, we have more time and energy to spend doing things together, and we let this time together change us for the better.

THERE IS A DIFFERENCE BETWEEN A NEED AND A WANT

As we practice more mindful consumption, we've shared more conversations about the difference between a need and a want. We are more inclined to examine what motivates us, to see where that could lead us, and decide if it's a worthwhile place to go.

OWNING LESS KEEPS THINGS MANAGEABLE

My oldest child, who is in middle school, has noticed more stress and confusion when her room is in disarray. She has seen the connection between not keeping more than she can manage and having more fun. Our children are learning not only to take care of their own possessions, but also to recognize how much they can manage, and how much is enough.

WE SET BOUNDARIES TO SERVE OUR PURPOSE

Our children have seen us turn down cool possessions and fun activities because we know that there is only so much we should take on. We need to know our purpose and how well another possession or activity lines up with that purpose.

Conclusion

I hope that I've helped you see that minimalism is a way of life and given you a proper introduction to its many benefits. I'm excited for you to start asking the questions that will help you define the boundaries of enough in your family's life and let you experience the joy of pursuing what matters most!

2 Becoming a Minimalist Family

Now that I've laid out what minimalism is and the benefits to living a minimalist lifestyle, I can talk next about how to become a minimalist family. Here's how to create a minimalist mindset, take first steps, and get your family on board.

Creating a Minimalist Mindset

Simplifying your home and life is one part perspective change and one part finding the practical method to get you there. The minimalist mindset is the fuel, and the method is the vehicle. You'll need both to go anywhere. I like to describe the minimalist mindset as a reduction of the inessential so that the essential may speak. It's a reduction driven by our own priorities. It's not about throwing everything out and then wishing you had a couch to sit on. It's about removing the inessential in your life so that you can see and have time for what is really important to you.

We may think we aren't defined by our stuff, yet many of us live as if we are. A minimalist mindset helps us see that possessions and busyness can too easily put us on a never-ending treadmill. Minimalism helps us take the time to think about what our culture tells us we should value and whether or not it will truly get us where we want to go. We don't have to live as if our inherent value is found in always having more. The minimalist mindset helps you stop making a living for all the things you don't really need, so you can use your resources to live your life.

Possessions are usually the first part of our lives we think about minimizing, and minimalism is partly about changing your relationship with your belongings. The truth is, most of us don't have an organization problem, we have an own-too-much-stuff problem. We try to get our house in order by organizing our things, but we're just moving them from one space to another, attempting to make our stuff look pretty. How much time do we want to spend making sure our things and our life look nice for others?

One of my favorite quotes about organizing stuff is from Joshua Fields Millburn, who says, "The easiest way to organize your stuff is to get rid of most of it." The best part of minimalism is letting it shape how you live your whole life. It's not a conspicuous lack of consumption—as if we gain status by demonstrating how little we can live on. A minimalist lifestyle just stops letting stuff—tangible and intangible—get in the way of a wholehearted pursuit of joy and contentment. Having an abundance mentality (acknowledging that our needs are met) helps us embrace gratitude.

First Steps

Clutter thrives in an environment of indecision. Here are the practical guidelines and steps that have helped my family cut through indecision and get the clutter out of our home. It is important to consider each of these as you work through each of your rooms.

KNOW YOUR WHY

Purging your possessions will be difficult at times—you're bound to hit physical and emotional road blocks. Knowing your *why* will help you keep your eyes fixed ahead on your goal. Your why is the fuel for the methods you adopt and adapt in pursuit of a minimalist lifestyle. When I first began this journey my why was less time taking care of stuff, and more time having fun with my family. This was my initial motivation, and it is still a part of my motivation for staying on this journey. As you continue, you may find, like I did, that your why changes and grows deeper with each layer of clutter you remove.

On a sheet of paper, write down your reasons for getting the clutter out of your home and life. It may seem like a trivial task, but there will most likely be times ahead when you feel defeated—and in those times you'll want to remember why you desire to live with less. Your why will help motivate you to continue on the minimalist path. When we're clear about our priorities and purpose, we can more easily discard whatever does not support them, whether it's clutter in our home or clutter on our calendar.

Sometimes we get so accustomed to living with cluttered rooms that we begin to overlook them and lessen our awareness of just how much the clutter affects our lives. With your why in place, it's time to see your stuff with new eyes.

DEFINE THE PURPOSE OF YOUR HOME

What is the purpose of your home? Most of us probably take this for granted—shelter, comfort, a place to be with family and friends, maybe a place to work or to enjoy a hobby. Know which purpose is most important for you and your family so that you can see how well that purpose is served. Prioritize the different ways you want your home to serve you and your family.

I want my home to be a safe haven, a place where we can connect and feel loved. I want it to be comfortable and beautiful, a place where rest is valued. If this is what I really want, I need to see how well my home meets these goals. If I don't prioritize these goals, I can get side-tracked by lesser goals—letting a home that displays current fashion take priority over a home that promotes comfort and rest.

I encourage you again to take some notes—on paper or digitally—of what you most want your home to do for you and your family, and do the same for each room in your home. Sometimes a room has more than one purpose, and that's okay. Places can be adapted to suit more than one purpose. Just watch out for lesser goals creeping in to the room's purpose—like giving storage more priority than it needs to serve your life.

DO MORE WITH LESS

As you enter each area, think of multi-functionality and reducing duplicates whenever possible. You might have five different tools for five different tasks that could all be done with one tool. As I sorted through my wardrobe and kitchen in particular, I was surprised at how many things I possessed that seemed redundant. Do I really need three different types of vegetable peelers? No, I think I don't. And in my wardrobe, do I really need the same style blouse in four different colors? No, I'm certain I do not.

Having a lot of choices for clothing means I need more closet space and more time to decide what to wear. Most single-use kitchen tools can be replaced with a knife (that you know how to use). I don't need to waste time looking for the singing pasta timer or that pale dogwood blouse. As you de-clutter you'll find that doing more with less feels much better than having more.

KEEP YOUR APPROACH AND EXPECTATIONS IN MIND

It helps to think about how you approach tasks. Are you an all-or-nothing or a slow-and-steady person? Recognizing this detail about yourself ahead of time will help set you up for success. This is true of family members as well.

Being someone who leans toward an all-or-nothing approach, I gravitated to places that I could de-clutter in one session. After I experienced the reward of a simplified space, I found more motivation to de-clutter places that would take multiple sessions to complete. Many places in my home have needed multiple sessions. I'm okay with this because I'm enjoying the rewards of our minimalist lifestyle. Setting yourself up to succeed is important. Reaching a goal without a lot of frustration motivates us to do it again.

As I mentioned, I lean toward an all-or-nothing approach. But with four small children, that typically just doesn't work out well. In the beginning, I made the mistake of expecting too much—too much from myself and too much from my family. The clutter bug had hit and I decided I wanted it all done, yesterday!

I realized that I couldn't accomplish all the de-cluttering I wanted to by myself and that—at least in the beginning—my family would not enjoy participating. So I began by defining an area I could do by myself in one session. This appealed to my "let's get this finished now" approach and let my family off the hook.

Accumulating your stuff was most likely a pretty gradual process. Getting rid of the excess will probably take more than a week, no matter which approach you take. Think about a large, one-time task that you've accomplished in the past—like moving. De-cluttering is like that task. Remember that your expectations need to match the size of the job you're facing, whether you're working alone or with your family. Unless you're okay living with more frustration and irritation for everyone involved, set reasonable expectations for yourself and your family.

SAY GOODBYE TO YOUR FANTASY-SELF AND SOMEDAY ITEMS

Our *fantasy-self* stuff often represents who we think we should be rather than who we are. But buying new photography gear isn't going to make you a photographer if your idea of taking pictures is always using your smartphone, just as buying another pair of running shoes isn't going to make you run a marathon if your idea of a workout is a walk around the block. While it is perfectly healthy to have goals and dreams, purchasing things will not bring that dream to fruition. In fact, all that fantasy-self stuff can keep you from achieving your goals. When you can say goodbye to your fantasy-self, you can say hello to your purpose and passion.

Do you find yourself hanging on to stuff because you might need it *someday*? It's easy to think that there may be a day when we will need our extra clothing or fancy dishes. But the truth is, that day will most likely never come and we can get by without it. It's time to break up with our someday stuff so we can better live today.

START SMALL

You might be overwhelmed by the state of your stuff. You look at it, unsure how you can de-clutter it all, and wonder where you should start—so many places to choose from! But where to start might not be the real problem, it just feels like it.

Getting stuff is typically associated with lots of good feelings—but getting rid of stuff, well, not so much. Why else would we have so much of it? So if you're stuck on where to start, don't be surprised. Just pick a smallish space.

It's perfectly okay to start small. If you start out tackling a big project, you're less likely to get the results you need to feel rewarded enough to do it again. You probably know how it feels to work away and have your task look undone (or maybe worse) when you're ready to quit. That feels like defeat—like you'll never get where you want to go.

Pick a small space. What matters most is that you actually *start*. Begin with something like your purse, the console of your car, your nightstand, the cabinet under your kitchen sink, or your kitchen utensil drawer. Maybe you feel excited about tackling a bigger space—your whole car or an entire room. Maybe it won't bother you at all to begin with a space you know you will not finish in one session. You may feel energized by this approach. But check in with other household members before you begin if your project involves any of their stuff or a shared space. And beware of not moving past the initial excitement of beginning your project.

I was able to gain some momentum when I started de-cluttering my own personal things. I was free to choose the fate of my stuff. No one had to give me permission to let go of 80 percent of my wardrobe, and no one objected. I worked with only my stuff and my space and avoided taking time away from routines my family and I enjoyed. Sorting first my own personal clutter built credibility and experience that my family could see. The start of persuading my family to join me in a minimalist lifestyle was letting them see me enjoy the fruits of my labor.

Whenever possible, set aside a specific block of time to de-clutter. It's hard to make progress on the fly when you're adopting a new lifestyle. A block of time along with some energy might come together unexpectedly, but probably not. Schedule some time when you will have a lot more energy than distractions. You will strengthen your motivation to continue as you set yourself up to succeed at small steps along the way. It really is true that little by little, a little becomes a lot.

CHOOSE A METHOD

To get started, you'll need to choose a method for de-cluttering that works for you. I've tried the four-box method, the packing party, and the sort-by-category methods, and all have worked well for me. Each method is a tool to help you see all of what you own and decide what to de-own and how to de-own it.

The four-box method takes you quickly to a decision: Give Away, Put Away (keep), Throw Away, or Not Sure. Use whatever containers work for you. If you use a floor or a table for uncontained piles, you will add another step to the process if you need containers to get the piles out of your home. I used this method and added a fifth category: Sell (until I ran out of stuff to sell).

When you're done sorting, choose a pile or box of belongings to Put Away, Give Away, Throw Away, or Sell. Set yourself up to keep going by choosing the pile or box containing the easiest category to deal with. If you're not sure which category that would be, ask yourself what will make you feel some sense of accomplishment with the least amount of effort (unless you enjoy doing the most difficult task first). Choose the approach that builds de-cluttering momentum for you.

There may be an approach that appeals to both you and another member of your household. Maybe your spouse or child would enjoy helping with a particular category of items. If not, that's okay. It's not worth dragging in unwilling participants. That builds resistance instead of momentum.

It might be helpful to put your Give Away items out of sight until you're ready to actually move them off your property or get them picked up. You'll immediately start enjoying the effects of less clutter. Just don't stop there—some of us are content to get these things organized and out of sight, and you might forget about these things until you open the drawer or the closet you put them in.

Avoid losing momentum here by knowing where to take (and leave) the Give Away items or when they can be picked up. Do some homework and research places that can use your donations before you begin your project in order to preserve your momentum. Find out what options are available in your community.

This applies also to your Sell items. Put them away until you're ready to sell them. Consider how you want to sell them: in a yard sale, online, or via a community tag sale (if your community offers one). If money gained from selling these items isn't adequate motivation for you to follow through with the work of selling, don't hesitate to move them into the Give Away pile.

Your Not Sure box may contain sentimental items that are difficult to let go of, things that are broken but maybe fixable and useful, or things that work just fine now and you might have a need for at some future point. Keep them tucked away and come back to them in the near future, or the not-too-distant future. As you get a little further along in your transition to a minimalist lifestyle, these things will get easier to deal with.

Throw Away items may or may not be the easiest to contend with. Can they go out with your regular trash? If not, what other choices are available in your community? You may need to schedule curbside pickup with your sanitation provider or find a way to get them to the local dump.

An adaptation of the four-box method is using only one or two of the boxes as you do an initial sweep of your lived-in spaces. Grab a bag and do a brief sweep through every room, picking up things to throw away or put away. Keep it simple and use whatever combination works for you. That might be just gathering up Throw Away items or Put Away items.

The packing party comes from The Minimalists, and it's a straightforward way to clear your home. Pack everything up as if you're moving. Label it all just as you would during a move: "living room," "kitchen utensils," "winter clothes," etc. Then spend the next few weeks unpacking only the items you need. By then you'll find you've only unpacked what you used. This method gets straight to identifying what you use regularly, and it quickly gives you more free space. At the end of the month, you will need to decide what to do with everything that remains packed in boxes. Having to sort through the boxes before de-owning them might tempt you to leave the items packed away. Be prepared to de-own everything left inside the boxes with no further sorting.

Sorting by category of item instead of by room has been made popular by Marie Kondo. It's usually referred to as the KonMari method. To get started, collect every single item you own of one kind and put them all in one big pile. For example, I gathered and set out every pair of shoes I owned. The next step is to hold each item with both hands and ask yourself if it sparks joy in you. If not, discard it. This method puts your focus on what to keep and tells you to thank the items that you discard for the work they have done in your life. The KonMari method also tells you to sort categories of things by a decreasing order of disposability. Clothing is first and sentimental items are last. In between are books, documents, and miscellaneous stuff.

When you see all of something that you own—such as shoes or handbags—it's usually a lot easier to determine what you want to keep and what you're willing to let go of. I found this approach very helpful because I didn't appreciate how many pairs of shoes I owned before I tried it. But for some, the thought of gathering certain things from all over your home, making a big pile of them, holding each one with both hands, and going through the entire pile in one sitting can be a deterrent to action. If that's the case for you, de-clutter by area until you get your possessions down to a more manageable amount.

SET LIMITS AND AVOID STORAGE

Although I'm not one to count my things or set arbitrary rules, it can be useful to set a numerical limit to the items you can own. You decide what number to use. And your "enough" limit is not set in stone. A minimalist lifestyle allows you the freedom to find what works for you and your family.

An "enough" limit can help you avoid purchasing more storage. Most often it's not more storage we need, it's less stuff.

WHAT TO DO IF YOU'RE INDECISIVE

Here are some options to consider when indecision strikes:

- **Take a break:** Your brain may just be tired of making decisions. Like physical exercise, it's a good idea to give our brains regular exercise followed by a break. When we made decisions to acquire more stuff, we most likely were not exercising our brain nearly as much as we are when we de-own it.

- **Go for a walk:** I've found taking a break and getting outside for some fresh air to be very beneficial! Do something you love that rejuvenates you—even if it's only for 15 minutes.

- **Ask yourself questions to help you decide:** Do I have more than one? Can it be easily replaced with something I already have? Could I borrow it? In what way does it simplify my life?

- **Remember your why:** If you continue to feel indecisive about an item, it may be helpful to remember why you chose to take the minimalist path in the first place.

KEEP THE CLUTTER OUT

How can we keep clutter from returning? Take care of the mail the day it arrives, if not as soon as you bring it in. Don't shop just for fun. Purge toys just before birthdays and holidays. Go for new experiences instead of new stuff. Make a place for everything you do have and make places for empty space just like you do for stuff. Some spots are magnets for clutter— improvise a way to stop clutter from getting back onto these magnet spots. Put things away at regular intervals—you choose how often that should be.

We often buy too much stuff because it's cheap and accessible— usually with a just a few mouse clicks. By choosing to spend more on higher-quality items, you can save money in the long run, and you also save the time you would otherwise spend shopping to replace the lesser-quality items that didn't last. Taking the approach of quality over quantity helps us stop purchasing cheap things that we don't need just because we can.

Getting Your Family on Board

In addition to reducing sentimental items, getting your family on board for your minimalist journey can prove to be quite a challenge. You may have just started or you may have begun simplifying years ago. Maybe you've read up on ways to reduce your wardrobe, tossed the expired medicine from 2005, and pared down your kitchen utensils. When I started de-cluttering six years ago, I was met with resistance from a few family members. Through mistakes I made, I quickly learned all the things that didn't work and what didn't convince them to get on board. In fact, my attempts to convince them cast their eyes farther away from seeing my point.

I never want my journey to simplify to become a wedge between me and what I value most, my relationships. When we have compassion and understanding for those we live with, we can hope to meet somewhere in the middle. Here's what I learned:

WALK THE WALK

Having a family usually means you not only live with other people, but you also live with all their stuff. Oftentimes it's other people's things that push our buttons more than our own clutter does, and it can be tempting to start minimizing with items that don't belong to you. But here's the thing: If you're walking the walk before you ask others to join you, you'll be familiar with the process of the change you're asking them to undertake—and you'll be better able to help the whole family move forward toward simplicity. Knowing the road ahead, understanding the difficulties, and achieving success yourself will help you help them. And the truth is, if you have not embraced a minimalist lifestyle, your children won't be able to follow suit.

SHARE YOUR WHY

Share with your family why you want to simplify. Tell them the *more* part about owning less. Help them understand that you want to simplify so that you can spend more quality time with them. Give them specific examples. Just before I started de-owing, I told my kids that we would have less time at the playground because it took us so long to find what we needed to get out the door—but once I got rid of some stuff and made our getting-out-the-door routine easier, we'd have more time outside. Maybe you want more family camping trips or more carefree Saturdays together. Whatever it is, share that why with them.

TELL THEM WHAT MINIMALISM IS NOT

Minimalism is not a contest to see who can live most miserably with the least amount of stuff. Relate minimalism to their specific life and give them examples. I might tell my eight-year-old son that minimalism does not mean he has to get rid of all his toys, but it does mean we want to keep the amount of his stuff manageable so we can spend more time swimming at the pool with friends.

MOTIVATE YOUR FAMILY

Motivating my family has been foundational to their embracing a less-is-more philosophy. Having open, consistent conversations is key to convey the benefits at hand in their daily lives. We have motivated our kids a few ways:

- **By giving praise:** I praise my children for their progress and attempts made, not for meeting my expectations. In other words, I avoid setting myself and my children up to be disappointed and possibly frustrating my family by keeping expectations out of the way. Some family members might never really be excited about a minimalist lifestyle, but I praise them for the efforts they make.

- **By offering rewards:** One of the benefits of minimalism has been using income that would have been spent on stuff to gift our family more experiences together. Treat your children to a fun experience after a de-cluttering day. Take a trip to the beach, the movies, a park, or a local festival. Give them a few options of things they'd enjoy and let them choose.

- **By focusing on the positives:** As you begin to see the benefits of minimalism in the lives of your children, point them out and high-light them. Do they have less laundry to put away? Do they have more time to play? Is it easier to find things? Encourage your children with the positive benefits that you notice in their lives.

- **By making it fun:** Although it takes a little bit of forethought, de-cluttering can be made fun for younger children. Set the timer, play some music, and turn the task into a game. (My main strat-egy to motivate my husband is less about fun and more about letting the benefits of my less shine through. He sees that I can find my things quicker and get dressed faster.)

- **By shifting the focus off stuff and on to experiences:** Look for everyday opportunities to shift your family's focus. My husband is retired Air Force and was deployed often. In the past, he would send the kids many toys when he was away, big ones to express how much he missed and cared for them. As our focus shifted, we shared with the kids that instead of daddy gifting them yet another stuffed animal, we would take a family trip upon his arrival home. Nearly every time, given the choice, our kids would choose an experience over another toy.

THINK ABOUT OTHERS

Get your family talking about other people—and what they can give to those people. I've shared the "Thankful Thread Challenge" with my children for the last few years. Conversations about the photos from *Where Children Sleep* has helped change their perspectives and open their hearts.

My family and I are fortunate to have more than enough and giving has been one of the most gratifying aspects of becoming minimalists. When my kids see us raise money for orphans, they want to give, too. Draw their attention to the needs of others and encourage them to give. Teach your children to use things and love people.

FOCUS ON WHAT TO KEEP

There are things that we know we don't want to keep anymore, but we still find ourselves owning too many things that we like. This is when it's essential to ask yourself, "What do I want to keep?" rather than, "What do I want to get rid of?" I found it most helpful to ask my children, too, what they wanted to keep rather than what they wanted to get rid of. Often, they would let go of more when we highlighted their favorites in each category. Focusing on keeping the very best helped them let go of the rest.

DISCUSS HOW THEY WANT TO LIVE THEIR LIVES

This past winter I brought my eight- and eleven-year-old to see a tiny home. They loved everything about it and were fascinated that this home could be transported to different locations. I could see the wheels turning in my eight-year-old's mind as he checked out the loft bed and the hidden kitchen drawers.

As we drove away from our tiny home tour he said, "Mom, that's what I'm going to live in when I grow up. I don't need a big house." Of course, he might change his mind later, but the seeds have been planted that bigger isn't always better and that less stuff equals more freedom to live the life he wants. A life spent on stuff is a life stuck on stuff—with little room for the things that matter. When your kids start talking about their dreams and aspirations, tell them how a balanced life with just enough stuff will help their dreams become a reality. Our children don't need to own more to be more.

EMPOWER KIDS

When I first started this journey, I wanted it all done quickly. I was frustrated by the state of our clutter, and the kids' toys were one of the first places I started to clean out. They were younger then, and I was able to part with much of their stuff without any fuss. But now that they're older, I let them decide what to keep as long as it follows our house guidelines. Allowing my children the opportunity to decide for themselves has empowered them to make decisions and has cultivated a sense of responsibility for their own things. In the beginning, they did not choose to donate as much as I wanted them to, but with consistency and patience they got better and better at letting things go that no longer served them.

GO SLOW

Teaching my kids and partner to become minimalists reminded me of the unseen or delayed benefits of parenting. You put in consistent effort as much as possible in hopes that fruit from your labor will grow in the future. It takes time to change, and I had to remind myself often that just because I saw the freedom in less didn't mean they would see it right away, too. Slow and steady makes change sustainable.

LET THEM STUMBLE

This goes along with empowering your children by allowing them to make their own decisions. But I want to carry it a step further—let them stumble through their decisions. If I decide everything for them, they won't have the skills to work through the process on their own. Last year, one of my children consistently complained about having to put away his clean laundry. He said to me in a whiny voice with his body flopping around like a wet noodle, "Mom, this is too many shirts to hang up." I reached deep down for the patience to say, "Yeah, you know…maybe this is too many shirts. Which one would you like to donate to a child in need?" He then decided he wanted to donate one shirt and hung the rest up without another word. I'd call that a win for everyone! When we let our children stumble in this journey, we're teaching them how to process decisions with a minimalist filter—one they can apply for the rest of their lives.

SHIFT THEIR PERSPECTIVES

When it comes down to getting your family on board with minimalism it's really about shifting their perspectives. This may mean offering more explanations and a new perspective when saying no to an item they want. I don't want to just tell them what to do all the time, I want them to see it for themselves, too. To do this, I keep communication open, free of criticism and judgment. I'm always looking for opportunities to highlight examples of living more from living with less.

Conclusion

Adopting a minimalist mindset is essential to reducing our excess and attaining lasting progress, for both you and your family. Now that we've set the foundation for developing a minimalist mindset, outlined first steps, and explored how to get your family on board, it's time to share the practical actions of becoming a minimalist family.

Part Two

Actions for Every Age

An entire family doesn't typically get on board with minimalism at the same time. Nevertheless, all families interested in minimalism need to communicate ideas about practicing minimalism now, even if those ideas aren't yet put into practice. In this section, I'm going to talk about helpful guidelines that you can discuss with your family members and implement in your home, as well as ways to manage resistance from your family.

3 Set Your House Guidelines

Over the last seven years I have removed thousands of items from our home and stopped more from coming in. We can de-clutter all day long, but if we don't develop habits that help us keep clutter out, we'll find our homes filling up again before we know it. It's just too easy to do. My hope is to present these guidelines in a way that helps you adapt them to your life. You'll likely find some more helpful than others, but it's hard to go wrong with my first one—value what you have.

Value What You Have

Every day we are flooded with advertisements that tell us we need something else or more of what we already have to be happy, beautiful, and successful. How often do we stop to remember that the primary driving force behind most ads is someone else's financial gain? It is sometimes very good and necessary to be driven by a belief that you need to be and have more. This drive in and of itself is not a bad thing—but it can be manipulated. When we really know what we value and value what we already have, then we're less inclined to go after more. Most advertising aims to unsettle our sense of contentment. Expressing gratitude is a way to talk back against the advertisements. We don't have to mindlessly go along with them. There are two ways that I've done this in my own life.

- **Express gratitude daily.** I've started intentionally expressing gratitude. Starting a gratitude journey, individually or with your family, is a great way to value what you already have. Gratitude opens the door to simplicity for your family. Spend time each day thinking about what you're grateful for.
- **Replace your "I want" with an "I have."** My minimalist journey has made me pay attention to my words about stuff. Take note when you start thinking about something you want. Be as clear as you possibly can to describe your desire. Then consider that you might already have something to meet this desire or that your desire simply will not be met by this new acquisition.

Stop Paying for Your Stuff

We pay for our stuff with time spent researching and shopping for the item, when we exchange money for it at the store, when we bring it home, and when we fix it or repair it. If you want to move forward in your de-cluttering journey, don't cling to a mistake just because you spent a lot of time making it, as a wise person once said. Allow yourself to stop paying for your stuff. By doing this, you're also making the choice not to fall into the eventual trap of obsessing over finding "the perfect home" for every item you originally acquired and now want to let go of. It's okay to spend some time researching places that will get your items to those in need, but don't let time spent doing this keep you from letting go of items until you find the perfect home. Depending on where you live, you may not have the most ideal option.

Follow the 80/20 Rule

The 80/20 Rule means that in any set of things—such as your possessions—a few (20 percent) are vital and many (80 percent) contribute very little. In other words, a few things make most of the difference. Applied to minimalism, it can be used to take stock of how many like items you actually use and compare that to the total number of those kinds of items.

If you have seven pairs of jeans and find that you nearly always wear the same two pairs, then those two are a vital part of your wardrobe. The other five pairs contribute very little, so you could sell or donate them. How easy is that? Not very for some. If it is easy for you, that's great! But if, after realizing that you rarely wear any of those five pairs of jeans, it's still not easy to de-own them, don't be discouraged or let guilt move in. Take time to look at your reasons for having those five pairs. What motivated you to acquire them? What are you hoping to accomplish by keeping them? Sometimes it's just having options that we really hate to give up, rather than any particular item. If that's the case for you, start to take note of what it costs to keep your options open. As I applied this principle to my belongings, I discovered that it generally holds true. My wardrobe, beauty products, books, and shoes all followed the 80/20 principle.

I wear the same clothes every week, apply the same beauty products, and wear the same shoes. I began to see that I could let go of many of my things and not even miss them. To discover how this principle might work in your life, consider packing up 80 percent of your beauty products or wardrobe. Set them aside in a box and live without them for at least a couple of weeks. After that time, you may learn there is indeed an item you truly need from the box or realize you can let it go happily.

Practice One Comes In, One Goes Out

This may not always be practical, but it's still a good guideline to help practice minimalism. Every time a new item enters your household, another item needs to leave. The rule is easiest to apply to similar items, but there could be times to apply it to dissimilar items.

In our home, we follow this guideline loosely based on the item and circumstance. With a minimal amount of stuff, I have the bandwidth and freedom to be flexible. I've found it works really well for smaller items like makeup, hair care items, and clothing. The goal is not a perfectly balanced equation, it's mindfulness of how much is coming in compared to how much is going out. The visible impact and success of this rule depends on where you are in your journey of de-owning.

The one-in-one-out guideline can also be applied to other areas of your life, like your calendar. Here's the thing about calendars—we can't create more hours in the day or more days on the calendar. And that's probably a good thing. When you add something new, decide if you should take something else away. If you've reduced the activities on your family's calendar to just enough, the one-in-one-out rule can help you maintain the balance.

Use It or Lose It

In our home, I like to call this the Use It or Give It guideline. If I'm keeping an item that isn't adding use or beauty to my life, why not give it away so that it can do that for others? Losing it is a loss but giving it is a gain.

This guideline can be applied to all of your stuff, and making the most of it means setting a useful time limit. For clothing, we donate what hasn't been worn in the last season. If I didn't wear a particular blouse or pair of shorts for an entire summer, I say goodbye to it. I might keep a swimsuit I didn't wear all summer if there were extenuating circumstances. I encourage our older children to be mindful of what they aren't using, and I try to be mindful of what my younger children aren't playing with.

Designate a Space

It's hard to keep what we don't have a place for. This has made off-property storage units a thriving business. Designate and define a space for each family member's things. Setting boundaries really does help us see what enough looks like. We don't have to set our boundaries in concrete, but they're a lot less useful if we change them every time the wind blows in another direction.

For example, our oldest son has a trundle under his bed where his toys are kept. He designated his trundle as the place for all his toys to live when he's not using them. We further defined this space by agreeing that the trundle must close easily when all of his toys are in it. This process is an opportunity for children to learn how to make more complex decisions, like what is worth keeping, and to enjoy the outcomes. Plus, he likes his toys kept out of sight from his younger brothers!

Other examples that you might find useful: designating a basket for stuffed animals, a cabinet for craft supplies, one closet rack for clothes, one drawer for cooking spices, and one drawer for kitchen utensils.

Put Away Used Items Each Day

Having a place for all of our stuff and putting it away when it's not being used is a recurring cost of owning stuff. If I haven't established a particular spot to keep my stuff and made a habit of putting it away, I will very likely spend more time and energy finding it when I need it or recovering from my irritation after I've tripped over it. So if I invest my time and energy toward making a habit of putting my stuff away every day—whether that's as soon as I'm done using it or before bed—I'm a lot less likely to get frustrated trying to find it or irritated by tripping over it. But I still need to invest my time and energy developing this habit. The less stuff I have to put away every day, the easier it is for me to habitually put it away every day.

Creating a family challenge can be a fun way to make this a habit. Each family member gathers their own items to see who finishes first or each one gathers only someone else's items to see who gathers the most. Another way to make this guideline work in your household is to choose the time of day that works best. I know I enjoy waking up finding things already in their place, so I routinely put stuff away in the afternoon or evening. I also enjoy making it easy to put things away as soon as I'm done using them.

Consider these four ideas to implement this guideline for your family. Every family member can help out and take responsibility for their belongings. Bring the whole family on board!

1. Return socks/shoes and backpacks to where they belong.
2. Take toys back to their proper places. Some days we don't have a clean playroom, but any toys brought to other areas in the home are returned to the playroom.
3. Do a room re-set. Each family member walks through their room and returns any items left out. If your young children aren't able to return items to their proper places, they can put them in a pile. Then you can help them return the items to their homes.
4. Set out clothes for the next morning and pick up any clothes left on the floor during the day.

It may take you a while in the beginning to complete these tasks, but they will move faster as you continue to purge the excess and implement this guideline in your home.

Gather Like Items and Choose One to Keep

During the initial purging of my closet, I was surprised by the number of like items I owned. I found lots of similar items in my closet that I made little use of. These items spent most of their time just taking up space. It was helpful to set a goal of identifying one or two of my favorites in any group of like items, keeping those and getting rid of the others. As I mentioned earlier, it's usually a more pleasant task to focus on what to keep rather than what to get rid of.

Using this guideline means gathering all like items throughout your home and putting them in one spot. Here are a few tips to make this task easier. Keep the goal in mind—identify only one or two favorites and stick to that number. Don't do this when you're feeling tired or stressed out, if possible. Avoid doing this when you would be subjected to a lot of distractions. And finally, decide exactly how you're going to de-own the not-so-favored items before you gather and choose. Making these decisions in the middle of this task will only slow you down.

Here are some ways we've used this guideline in our wardrobes: I kept only one black dress from the four I owned; reduced four black belts down to two; reduced eight pairs of jeans down to two; reduced five coats down to three—one for fall, one for winter, and one rain coat; and reduced a suit collection from eight to three (and the three are versatile so they can be worn at any occasion).

Finish Each Job You Set Out to Do

As much as possible, complete each task—completely. Finishing a task feels great. But finishing a task is hard. Putting your stuff into different piles or containers according to how you will de-own it might be easy, but actually getting rid of stuff can be difficult when we don't realize how much time and energy it will take to accomplish this. Avoid starting with lots of enthusiasm and energy only to finish with unwelcome fatigue and a sense of failure. You might not be inclined to try again; the thought of this scenario might keep you from even starting.

Make it more possible to complete the task you set out to do. As I mentioned before, set yourself up to succeed. Finishing what you set out to do nearly always feels good enough to make you want to come back and do it again. So before you set out to de-own a lot of your stuff, test the waters first. Make your first project a small one. There will likely come a time when you need to accomplish a big project that you can't break up into smaller steps over several sessions. But it's perfectly okay to start with an easy-to-manage project.

Set Guidelines for Gifts

One of the challenges families face when pursuing minimalism is what to do about the gifts that come with birthdays and holidays. It doesn't matter where we are on the path of minimalism; we need to *stay* on it. Receiving gifts can present us with a detour that needs to be negotiated.

ADOPT A MINIMALIST HOLIDAY MINDSET

One of the biggest hurdles for families can be adopting a minimalist mindset regarding holiday gifts for their family and other loved ones. Although it's perfectly okay to celebrate a holiday without presents, most people exchange gifts as part of many different holiday celebrations. Minimalism and gift exchange are not mutually exclusive. A minimalist holiday mindset in our home is about taking the focus off of gifts and putting it back on other things, like family and community.

My best holiday memories are centered around faith, family, friends, and traditions, not around the gifts I received. We can mindfully redefine the way we celebrate holidays and center them around the things that truly matter—which in my life are pretty much not things.

We exchange less time shopping for more and more time with family and friends. I like to say that "we prefer your presence to your presents." We exchange a few gifts during holidays, but we don't let this part of our celebration take center stage.

It can be hard to think clearly as we set out to find gifts during holiday seasons. Advertising is ramped up several thousand notches. We may believe that the holidays can't be celebrated without gifts, so we feel pressure to find gifts to give. If you want to buy gifts, choose them before the holiday season sets in. Applying mindfulness means we think before we buy.

EXPLAIN YOUR NEW DIRECTION IN GIFTING

As you share with your family your desire to live a minimalist lifestyle, talk about the impact of receiving gifts. Will the gift be useful? Where will you put it? How long does the initial excitement of receiving a gift last? Talk about the pressure from advertising and traditions that impel us to exchange gifts. (Conversation kept free of accusations and judgment will go much further.) Talk about different ways to share time with other people without exchanging gifts. Discuss what you'd like to do in place of exchanging gifts, and note that there is still room in your life for gift exchange—like a shared experience.

MAKE YOUR GIFT REQUESTS KNOWN EARLY

Give your wish-list to thoughtful gift givers ahead of time. Provide them with a specific list of experiences. Let them know what you and your family members enjoy. Find opportunities to let your family and friends know that you prefer experiences over traditional gifts. This is part of the joy of being together!

GIVE EXPERIENCES

Give experiences rather than stuff. Just as we choose experience gifts as much as possible, we like to give experience gifts as well. Not only does this type of present keep the clutter out for others, but it also provides people with a new way of connecting. We've given experience gifts for several kinds of occasions: Christmas, birthdays, going-away parties, and more. Some experiences we've found worth gifting are your time, a home-cooked meal, a letter of appreciation, breakfast in bed, childcare or other respite care, tickets to a concert, and a class related to a hobby.

FOCUS ON GIVING

The saying "'Tis better to give than to receive" holds true. We can see our abundance as an opportunity to give in abundance. Consider donating to a charity on behalf of your loved ones and invite your family members to do the same. Rather than asking your child for their Christmas wish-list, ask them to make a Christmas wish-list of things to give. Invite your children to write down gifts they'd like to give to others during the holiday season. Maybe they can help a neighbor, donate toys, write a thank-you note to a member of the military or a veteran, or serve together at your local food pantry. By asking our kids a different question, we can watch their hearts and minds shift from a focus of what they can get to what they can give. When our children know they have something of value to share, I believe they are more able to find—and share!—the joy of a healthy and loving community.

ANNOUNCE A NO-GIFT POLICY

Include a message in your party invitation that lets your guests know you're celebrating without gifts. A simple message like: "No need to bring a present, please, just your presence!" or "As appreciated as your gifts may be, they are not needed as you will see."

Another idea for no-gift parties is to invite your guests to donate to their favorite charity as a present, or suggest a charity that is meaningful to your family. You could also invite guests to exchange one gift (an experience) at your party so that everyone receives just one present. It can be difficult to change traditions, but starting small often leads us to the result we want eventually.

I have been to no-gift parties at which some people did bring gifts. I know it can feel awkward arriving at a party empty-handed while others bring wrapped gifts. But I encourage you, if the invitation says no gifts are needed, do not bring a gift. I'd rather honor the host's request and trust them at their word than bring a gift just so I don't look or feel awkward.

HANDLE UNWANTED GIFTS

There will be people in your life who hear your simplicity message and honor your no-gift requests. And there will be people you love and who love you who will not understand your requests for less. When those people who don't hear me (for whatever reason) give me more gifts, I warmly accept the presents and thank them. After that, I may keep the gift for a day or a year, but ultimately the gift has been given and I'm free to do with it as is best for my life.

When I've been given and accepted a gift I no longer want, I make one of two choices depending on the relationship. One is to go to the gift giver and explain that while I appreciate this useful/beautiful/helpful item they thoughtfully gave me, it isn't serving its purpose in my home—and I just haven't been able to use it or find a spot for it. I ask them if they would like to have the item and if it would be helpful in their life. Most often people will give you permission to give the item away.

If your loved one becomes offended and upset that you don't want the gift, kindly remind them that your intent is not to upset them and that you appreciate their thoughtfulness. But you want the item to actually be used and appreciated. Just as they enjoy giving you things, you enjoy giving other people things you don't need in this season of your life.

The other option is to simply donate it without talking with them about it. This option is easier when you've been given gifts from people you don't have ongoing close relationships with. When my children received gifts from their no-gift birthday party, we donated them to a local charity. My kids and I had a discussion about what to do before the party. I explained that people would, in their own way of thoughtfulness, most likely bring gifts despite what the invitation said and that they could choose to keep them or donate them. Five out of six gifts my daughter willingly chose to donate. She has learned to ask good questions, the right questions, about the cost of ownership, and she's learning to identify things that are in excess of her needs. Accepting the gift with gratitude and choosing not to keep what she didn't need was her opportunity to give to others.

REMOVE GUILT FROM THE EQUATION

Most often when a gift giver gives you something, they sincerely believe it's the right thing to do, whether or not it adds practical value to your life. A gift is usually meant to confer some honor and respect, even if it is not something you want to keep. Remember that when a gift is given to you, you can decide whether to keep it or let it go.

Conclusion

We can de-clutter all day long, but if we don't develop habits and guidelines that help us keep clutter out, we'll find our homes filling up again before we know it. Keep these guidelines near. Write them down and place them where your family can see them. Continue using them, since they'll help your family continue moving forward toward a minimalist life.

My hope is not that you follow these guidelines like a rulebook but more a fluid document—using and applying them in ways that work best for your family.

4 When You Encounter Resistance

If some members of your household are not interested in minimalism, be prepared to meet resistance. Instead of resenting its appearance, see it as a challenge to negotiate and navigate. Look for ways to soften resistance, and if that doesn't get you where you want to go, then look for ways around it.

Approaching Resistance

My husband and I have different opinions, interests, and hobbies. It's part of what makes our family a beautiful unit—we're often introducing one another to different things. My husband is the early-rising list maker and I'm the mid-morning list thinker. Our daughter is into making movies, and our boys are into crazy contraptions built with kitchen utensils, paper clips, and rubber bands. We all enjoy different things and have different interests.

My husband and I seemed to be pretty much on the same page as we began our minimalism journey. Disagreements about what and how much to let go of came up when I set out on a major purge. I wanted to remove 70 percent of our possessions and he wanted me to stop at a 40 percent reduction. Since I knew that actually implementing minimalism would be done by me, I made the decision to be okay with that and de-clutter at a rate that was a compromise between my husband's goals and mine. As time and the layers of our things were peeled back, he's come along and joined me.

Here are the strategies that I've used to pursue minimalism while living with family members who do not share my enthusiasm.

JOIN A COMMUNITY

I cannot emphasize enough the value of being connected to a like-minded community focused on simplicity and intentional living—especially when there isn't anyone in your home or local community to offer support, ideas, or encouragement. There will be days when you feel defeated, alone, and misunderstood in your pursuit to live more intentionally with less stuff—and a minimalist community is a valuable resource where you will find the encouragement needed to move forward.

A few of the most encouraging Facebook groups I'm a part of are the No Sidebar Community, Simple Collective from The Art of Simple, and Joshua Becker's private Uncluttered Facebook group for those enrolled in his Uncluttered Course. These groups are a place for you to further connect for encouragement and explore how minimalism and simplicity can look in your life. If you're not already a part of these groups, I encourage you to check them out.

HIGHLIGHT THE BENEFITS OF YOUR VISION

My vision of simplicity includes my family—all of us together—reducing the clutter so we can live a more intentional and meaningful life. This means that when they resist, the most helpful thing I can do at this point is show them the benefits that are specific to them—to what matters in their life. Although a sit-down chat to remind my family of the mutual benefits can be helpful, I've had more success wooing them by sharing small nuggets of the benefits in their life.

For example, my husband had boxes of awards, certificates, and gifts from his 20-year career in the Air Force. It's the kind of meaningful stuff that he didn't want to just get rid of but also didn't want displayed in our living room. So it sat in boxes for years. The next time we talked about the boxes, I took that opportunity to tell him how tossing them would benefit our family. I explained that when we're gone, the kids won't know any of the stories behind his awards, medals, or certificates from deployments to Africa, Kuwait, and Iraq. I suggested we take a picture of each item and include a short story with it. He could keep it as a digital collection or put physical photos with their stories in one binder. He agreed this was a much better way to share his memories without the heavy burden of stuff!

For my children, I talk about the benefits in our everyday conversations. They might hear me say "I'm glad we don't have too many things to tidy up around the house—we'll be able to get to the pool sooner." Or, "It's great that with your room uncluttered we can set the tent up in it for your friend's sleepover." With consistent conversations highlighting the benefits of minimalism in their life, minimalism gets gently woven into their mindset. Occasional sit-downs can be helpful, but it's the subtle consistency that will really sway them.

MODEL MINIMALISM

I think the best way to draw people into minimalism is to live your own minimalism and to do it joyfully. It's easy to be discouraged when those we love refuse to simplify along with us. And it's easy to underestimate the power you have to make a difference. You can deflect negativity and emphasize the positive aspects of minimalism as you focus on your why for becoming minimalist. You can choose to bring more kindness, generosity, resilience, and perseverance to your family's minimalist life than those around you—even despite those around you. Keep working toward your goals in any area you can.

When you're making tangible progress with your own stuff, it will show. Let time speak for the changes you're making. This will be far more convincing than telling family members that they need to, or ought to, or just have to de-clutter their wardrobe. While my husband still stared into his full closet of clothes but had nothing to wear, I was already dressed and ready to go. While my husband searched for his shoes under his clothes he didn't wear, I slipped mine on my feet. Through experiences like these, my husband began to see just how much our clutter cost. He realized how much our excess took away from the things in our life that hold real value. When you encounter resistance, sometimes the best thing to do is quietly and subtly show the positive effects of minimalism.

DO NOT DISCARD OTHER PEOPLE'S THINGS WITHOUT THEIR PERMISSION

There is no quicker way to kill your message of simplicity than by starting to toss other people's possessions without their permission. In our home, everyone has the opportunity to choose the fate of their belongings, even our small children. I never want my children to fear that one day they'll come home and their things won't be there. I respect their feelings and their right to choose. When we discard people's things without their permission, we give them reasons to hang on to their stuff with an even tighter grip. Of course, there are times when we as the parents must set spatial boundaries—but even in this case we can give our children the opportunity to choose their favorites.

DON'T FORCE MINIMALISM

Focus on your own minimalist journey. Share it with your family. Share it with your community. But resist forcing it on others or, even worse, judging them. People do not make permanent and sustainable changes just because someone else tells them to. If they want to keep something, be agreeable. Let them know you'd rather cut the clutter and part with it, but you will honor their request to keep it. Dictating what items they may keep will only bring resentment.

If You Hit a Brick Wall

There are times when our efforts and goals are not embraced by those we live with, when our partner or other adult family member is unwilling to participate in any move toward minimalism. If this happens to you, there are ways to keep the peace and still move yourself into minimalism. Consider these tips to find common ground and keeping moving forward.

REQUEST ONE ROOM

If your adult family member is a packrat, hoarder, or avid shopper who prefers stuff over space, ask them for one room that you can make your own. Clear out as much as you need to in this room so you have someplace where you can enjoy a minimalist environment. Let everyone else in your family see you enjoy this space, and don't be surprised if other family members want to start spending more time in it, too!

GIVE THEM SPACE

Giving your partner or other adult family member their own space can be reassuring to them—especially if they already feel like you're out to toss all their stuff. Give them a space where they can keep things as they wish. As you pare down other areas of the home, they may be more inclined to join you in your efforts in those rooms. For example, maybe your partner stacks papers on the kitchen counter. Offer them a different space to put those papers—a basket, tray, cabinet, or even a drawer that you cleared out. This works best if they feel that using the new location is at least as convenient as putting their papers on the kitchen counter. Do we want to keep stacks of papers? No, of course not. But if it's their stuff, better to compromise with small areas so you can free up most of the space in the room.

SET FAMILY REWARDS

Give rewards to family members who take de-cluttering steps with you. Make the connection between the task and the reward easy to see. If you've de-cluttered the kitchen together, make their favorite meal or snack to celebrate. Let them know how much easier it is to cook in an uncluttered space. If you've de-cluttered the living room together, celebrate with movie night or game night in that space. Let them know how much you love spending time together in an unclut-tered space.

Conclusion

Navigating any relationship takes a lot of patience and creative compromise. You are only in control of yourself. In the end, the positive behaviors that you display will likely inspire others to make positive changes as well, even if they initially resist.

As you set out to apply your house guidelines, keep in mind the ages of everyone in your family. Different ages are capable of different levels of simplifying, and different aged children will resist in their own ways. And be sure to revisit the guidelines and strategies to manage resistance from family members as your children age. You may need to adjust your guidelines or even adopt new techniques as your children grow older.

Even if your entire family isn't following your minimalist path at the same time, continue using these guidelines and strategies. Most of all, continue your own journey to minimalism as inspiration and motivation for them to join you!

Part Three

Clean Up and Clear Out: Strategies For Every Room

In this section, I will address the rooms in your home and show how to transform each one into a minimalist sanctuary. A minimalist home doesn't need to be all white and sleek with modern furniture. There doesn't have to be a particular limit to the square footage or the number of possessions you own. My hope is that you will find here practical strategies that let you discover and create a home that has only what serves you well, and nothing that distracts you from what you really want.

5 Living Areas

It will be helpful to have the First Steps section from Chapter 2 (page 18) fresh in your mind as you start each room. As you look at the items you keep in your living areas, ask yourself questions like: What purpose does this serve? How is it being used? What do I accomplish with it? Do I enjoy looking at this, and how often do I notice it? See your home as a place for people to unwind and engage with one another, and look for anything that hinders that.

Remember to start with your own things. Depending on your inclination to take risks and your allotted time, you can go for what's easiest or least difficult to let go, or you can remove a bit more than you're comfortable doing and see if the new space gives you more peace than the removed item did.

Before you begin, get your four-box method sorting station set up—this will enable you to de-clutter items without making immediate decisions. Also look for social services, non-profit organizations, and consignment shops in or near your community that take donations. I have donated items to Goodwill, Operation Give, Vietnam Veterans of America, and local shelters for people and animals.

Furniture

Furniture is often among the largest and most costly of your home purchases, and the price you paid for a piece of furniture might be the only thing that keeps you hanging on to it. But the truth is, when you keep what will not get you where you want to go, you're still paying for it. The price of any possession that costs you your peace is too high. You can't move forward until you cut your loss and let it go. And you won't be done paying for that piece of furniture until you pick it up and move it out yourself, or make a plan for someone else to do that for you—even if you have to pay them!

Take notice of the fit and flow of furniture in each room. Can you gain some free space without compromising how well the room functions for you and your family? Removing even one piece of furniture can bring a room to life by giving you more space to breathe. If the room or space feels empty after removing an item in question, I encourage you to leave the new space open for at least a few weeks. You might need, as I did, more than a few minutes or a day to notice a connection between more empty space in your home and more peace of mind.

Align your furniture needs to your family's lifestyle. A family with several children and a family that loves to entertain may need multiple couches, while a family of three and a family that doesn't host large groups might only need one.

Does your dining room hold more chairs than people in your home? If so, are the chairs ever used? Ask yourself these kinds of questions about each piece of your furniture: What is it used for? How much space does it occupy? Could a smaller piece do the work of the larger piece (not that you must make that exchange now, but keep it in mind for the time you are ready to replace a large piece)? Again, the goal is not to own only a certain number of pieces of furniture, but to turn our focus back to people and away from our possessions.

To get you thinking, ask yourself if you really need any of these particular pieces of furniture. We want our guests to have a place to sit, but if you're holding on to chairs that haven't been sat on for a year, chances are they aren't needed.

BOOKSHELF

If keeping a large collection of books, DVDs, CDs, or framed photos adds value to your life, you're likely to have a bookcase or two in your home. As our journey continued, we donated and went digital with many of our collections that lived on our bookcases. It can be tempting to continue holding on to various shelving units even after you've donated the items that sat on them—after all, we've believed it's more and better storage we need, rather than less stuff. You might think about finding another purpose for the bookcase; just be sure that the new purpose meets your need for more free space and fewer things to care for. An unfilled bookcase is typically a magnet for clutter—it's just too tempting to place things there.

BUFFET OR DINING ROOM HUTCH

Before becoming minimalist, I acquired my grandparents' dining hutch, dishes, and crystal. I enjoyed using the hutch along with the table linens and crystal that my grandparents had kept in it. But after several moves, I could see that I hardly used the linens or the crystal and had no other use for the hutch. I was a little sad to see it go because it was a part of the many meals I enjoyed with my grand-parents. But the hutch, crystal, and linens were just accessories to that enjoyment and those memories, not necessities.

TV STAND OR ENTERTAINMENT CENTER

You can choose to ditch this piece of furniture altogether by saying goodbye to your television, or just hang your TV on a wall. We had a TV stand up until a few years ago. Hanging the TV on the wall was easier than we thought. If you can't hang your TV on a wall, choose a low-profile piece for it that will not hold anything else, or choose a piece that serves another necessary purpose. Plan to make it difficult, if not impossible, for this piece of furniture to turn into a clutter magnet.

DISPLAY CABINETS

Display cabinets are usually large pieces of furniture used to hold more things. Ask yourself if your life is made better (brought joy and purpose) by placing items on display. If so, you know they are worth keeping. If not, ask yourself how much time, energy, and space you are using to keep this display. A good part of your time and energy cost may well be keeping clutter off of this piece of furniture. Display cabinets often occupy a lot of space for a small return. If the cost of maintaining the items is too high, get rid of both the items and the display cabinet.

COFFEE TABLES

These are often used to display decorations or magazines rather than hold a cup of coffee. If having drinks in the living room is important, look for other options that take up little space and are easy to place where they work best. Pick one piece of furniture to accomplish your goal. If you have an end table and a coffee table, ask yourself if you can accomplish your goal with one or the other. In addition, think about using furniture that serves two functions. In the past we've set up a beverage station for guests on a kitchen counter, dining room table, and small portable table we borrowed. We gave up our coffee table years ago and I haven't missed it one bit!

CORNER TABLES

The entryway table by the front door, the table in the corner of the dining room with a plant on it, and the sofa table all occupy space with little return for your investment. You may have them because they look good and you felt like you had to fill these spaces, but if the sight of any of these tables doesn't make you smile and relax, then are they really looking good enough to keep? Maybe you don't actually need to fill that space.

This is just a short list to get you thinking outside the box. But no matter what you do, furnish only with what fits your lifestyle—not your neighbors' lifestyles or a lifestyle you see in a simple living magazine. It's your living room, so make it work for you.

Décor

Consider this thought: You don't have to fill every space with a treasure—maybe the clear space itself is the greater treasure. As you look around at your home décor, do you see things in places because you feel like you have to fill those spaces? If so, consider removing them. As we simplify our home décor, we can keep items we love and let them stand out while we still have space for clear thinking and relaxation.

With décor, starting from empty can help you identify what brings beauty. You can start with a blank slate by removing all the decorative items from your living space. Define the space to be occupied by decorative items before you begin putting anything back. How do you want the space to look? How much free space are you aiming for? Put back only what you really love, and put back pieces one at a time. Give priority to your favorite decorative items that are well made and built to last. Besides being better for our planet, this can save you decision-making time and energy in the future.

Décor trends change often, and you may find that you change your mind about what decorative items bring beauty and enjoyment to your home. Becoming minimalist doesn't mean you can never change your home's décor. But it does mean that you consider the time and energy you've already spent creating free space in your home, as well as the time, energy, and money you will spend shopping, choosing, and perhaps second-guessing your decisions. Always ask yourself how this investment brings you more of what matters most in your life.

If the items you have removed have left empty space, live with that simpler space—even with some empty walls—for at least a week. Live with it long enough to feel confident that you no longer need an item hanging on that wall, or until you're sure you've found something that brings you joy. There is growth when we let less grow on us—saving our resources for more important goals.

Electronics

Simplifying our electronics isn't just a way to reduce clutter, it's essential to the health of our family. We live in an attention economy—we spend our attention to consume information. A minimalist approach to electronics in our family is about learning how to guard our attention from this barrage of constant screen chatter, as well as having mindfulness about what we are consuming. Setting electronic boundaries—which can include a periodic fast from social media—will help us guard our attention. Here are a few ways we've applied this in our home.

- **Pare down devices.** Consider allowing no more than one device per family member and think about if small children need any devices at all. When we limit our devices, we're saving ourselves time and money and cutting off opportunities to waste our time.
- **Designate a charging and resting station.** Just as our bodies should rest, so should our devices. Consider setting up a charging station (preferably not where you sleep) where all devices can be left. Building this into your family's routine forces family members to take electronic breaks and fosters better connections.
- **Resist the impulse to upgrade.** The enticement to upgrade is not necessarily all about having the latest and greatest model. Part of the enticement is in the upgrade moment itself. It's similar to those times when our children know they're getting a new toy. They don't even know what the toy is and yet they are still excited. We, too, can get excited about the acquisition of something new. Typically, we're already excited about upgrading before we know much of anything about the new device. Don't let this excitement impair your decision making. Upgrading your electronics every time a new model comes out could downgrade your quality of life, as well as our planet.

HOW TO DISPOSE OF ELECTRONICS

For your computer or laptop, consider upgrading some of the hardware or software or adding external storage before you decide to dispose of it.

If you decide not to upgrade your electronics, you can find places to recycle or donate them. If your item is damaged, look for an electronics waste recycler in your area. Call2Recycle offers drop-off locations for rechargeable batteries and cell phones all over the United States. For larger items, check with your local town, city, or county government for special collection or drop-off days. Every Best Buy store takes back electronics to recycle. Staples also takes back many electronics for free recycling. You can find updated information about recycling your electronics at the Electronics TakeBack Coalition website.

If your item is in working condition, consider donating it; there are many charities and non-profits that will gladly take it. One option is Dell's Reconnect program, a partnership with Goodwill that accepts any brand of computer or anything that can be connected to a computer.

Be sure to wipe all of your information off your devices before recycling or donating them.

Keepsakes and Sentimental Items

The questions I've suggested you ask when choosing what stays and what goes typically don't work well when going through your sentimental things. After all, we're inclined to keep these items even if we have no use for them, if they're broken beyond repair, or if their style no longer suits us. When we look at these items, a special memory or a whole set of special memories often come to mind. De-owning a sentimental item can feel as if we're losing a part of our self. It's a good idea not to begin your de-cluttering journey with these items. Even after you've made a successful first pass through your fantasy-self things and perfectly good items, meeting up with your keepsakes so that you can thin them out might feel like walking into a wall.

With marriage, motherhood, and moving due to the military, I had grown and so had my family. Possessions I once held dear started to loosen their grip as the meaning behind the keepsake moved from the item to my heart. I didn't need to hold on to my grandparents' dining hutch to remember and honor them. And I discovered that their love and legacies were never in their dining hutch anyway; they were always in their characters. It is possible to peel away the layer of heavy sentimental items that weighs you down. Through the years, I learned how to simply let go of things that were too heavy to hold as I moved forward.

SHIFT YOUR PERSPECTIVE

Our perception can become our reality. How we see something becomes our truth, which at times can be self-limiting. When our focus is on the past or the future, it's usually at the expense of the present. When we shift our perspective to the present, we give ourselves permission to let go of the heavy sentimental things that are no longer serving us in the here and now.

TAKE PICTURES

Take photos of the sentimental things weighing you down. Make a digital photo book that tells their story. My husband realized the importance of this when I reminded him that our children would have no idea what his awards from his military career meant if he kept them stuffed in a box. Our kids would most likely just see boxes of things they'd have to get rid of later on. As mentioned earlier, my husband took photos of his memorabilia and put them in an album that we can all enjoy.

My children have also embraced the idea of taking a photo of artwork they have created that they want to remember. They know that if we kept everything, we'd spend time caring for their creations rather than having time to make more. They are learning that it's hard to make new memories if you're always living in old ones.

CULL KEEPSAKES FROM YOUR CHILDREN

When my children handcraft something for me—such as a pottery dish from art class at school—I may keep it indefinitely or just for a short while. They know I may not keep it forever and they offer me the same freedom I've given them—they never have to keep something just because I gave it to them. I've shared with them through many conversations that my love is not inside the gift, my love is the gift, and no material thing will ever change that.

I have one small container where I keep a few things they have given me. But since becoming minimalist it's never been full, and I periodically revisit my desire to keep each item in it.

ASK YOURSELF QUESTIONS

Sometimes the easiest way to determine what to keep and what to get rid of is to ask yourself simple questions. Try these questions on for size when considering what to do with keepsakes:

- **What do I need during this period of my life?** No matter what items you're holding on to, make sure they allow you to move in the direction that you want to go.
- **What do I want to keep?** When you're trying to let go of sentimental things, focusing on what you're giving up can make the task much more difficult. If you have 25 sentimental items from a loved one, decide how many you can keep without weighing

yourself down. Do you want and need all 25? If so, consider the cost of keeping these things in terms of your finite resources of time, emotional energy, and space.

- **Do I want to leave this for my family?** Consider parting with keepsakes and heirlooms that have become heavy, not just for the sake of your own journey but also as a gift for your loved ones. They will not have this burden to carry or unload on their journeys.

Books

Books can be another sticking point for some of us. Here are some helpful questions to ask yourself about your books (or CDs or DVDs). Why do you keep them? Do you keep them to read, do you keep them to look at, or both? Do you relax when you look at them? Do you relax when you look at books you haven't read yet? How much of your identity are you placing in the books? What else could you do with this space? You could box up the books and give yourself time to see how the new empty space makes you feel.

If you truly enjoy having books in your home, identify your favorites. When you ask yourself which ones you want to get rid of, you will most likely end up with a small pile—but when you ask yourself which ones you need and love most, you'll know which ones you could happily live without. Again, define a space for books before you choose your favorites.

You can donate books to libraries, schools, hospitals, and shelters. When I lived in Connecticut, a group of moms gathered up books from other families in the community to give to a nearby school that needed them. Identifying places that can use your books and then delivering them can strengthen your connection with your community. Another way to strengthen your connection with your community is to join and use your local library. Most books that are not already in place can be ordered, and many books can be borrowed online. On another front, having a book exchange every few months is a terrific way to stay connected with old friends and meet new ones.

For those who love reading from a real paper book—I hear you! But when possible, choose digital options to save on space and paper waste. There are so many devices and digital ways to read books. You might prefer a device like a Kindle that can be used just for reading. My mom has kept her Kindle for six years because it helps keep her away from online distractions.

Photographs

After my grandparents passed away in 2006, my mom and I went through their belongings together. We sorted through hundreds of photos. Some were kept in old photo albums (the photos were deteriorating) while others were in the form of slides. We gathered them up and had them digitally scanned before they were no longer recognizable. By scanning them we were able to share them online and on a disc with other family members.

If you're like I was, you'll have printed photos stored in various places around the house that are not being displayed. Gather all your loose photos into one location. Next, sort your photos into categories. As you sort photos into categories, don't spend too much time getting stuck on what to keep.

After all photos have been sorted, pick out your favorites and discard the rest. I stored the keepers in a simple photo storage box and used index cards to separate the years. Photo negatives and slides are best stored flat. If you find photos you want to keep even though they aren't favorites, consider keeping them as digital files only. If you really enjoy keeping physical photo books, define a space for where you will keep them. Be mindful of why you keep these and whether they hinder or help your life's journey.

Later I ended up scanning all of my photos, keeping only digital records of all of them. Consider scanning all your physical photos and discarding the ones not being displayed. You can invest in a digital frame to display hundreds of photos. These digital frames can play a slideshow of the photos of your choosing. We had one in the past and our kids loved looking at the photos filled with fun times we've had together. Keep in mind that as our digital presence increases, so does our photo collection. In fact, I ended up hoarding photos on my computer! The cost of film, its processing, and storage space are no longer limiting factors. Use the same principles to simplify your digital photos that I talked about for your physical photos.

Special Spaces for Your Kids

As you start de-owning your excess you may begin to see that your child's things are spread all throughout the house. Our kids do not have to have a space for their things in every room—in fact, that may not be beneficial for anyone in your family. Setting up a dedicated children's space—whether it's a playroom, craft table, or reading corner—can facilitate playing and learning without clutter and chaos.

I'm a big fan of independent play. A child-friendly space—such as a chalk wall for young children or a bedroom for older children—will keep you or another adult from managing their stuff directly or constantly directing them to manage it. Don't get distracted by the "cool" or "wow" factor when you create this space. Think more about how well it will serve everyone's needs. Remember, you're after more free and creative play for the kids and more time for you to enjoy seeing them play!

As you decide how to keep your children's things from being scattered about your home, here are some tips to keep in mind.

- **More sharing.** Whether you have one child or more than one, you may want to have only one special indoor play space. Having fewer toys and spaces to claim as their own actually promotes sharing. With the exception of choking hazards or special toys, all of our kids can play with any toy that isn't currently being played with. One child may ask a sibling to give them a toy that their sibling is using, though they have to honor a "no" and wait until their sibling voluntarily gives it up. I do not force them to share. This gives them plenty of opportunity to develop their social skills.

- **More creativity.** When you set out to simplify a space for your child, having just enough stuff will foster greater creativity. Your child's space does not have to contain every toy designed to entertain, rather than innovate. Keeping their space simple will allow more room for their imagination to grow.

- **Greater purpose.** When we apply minimalism to our child's special space we remove whatever distracts us from our goals for them. Keep your goals in mind: independent and free play, creativity, sharing, socializing, and the opportunity for you to watch them grow!

SPACES FOR TODDLERS AND PRESCHOOLERS

Is your toddler's space for playing, resting, or learning? Maybe it's one large space for all of those things. I like to call our toddlers' play space a "yes" zone. If I want to provide an environment that cultivates learning, connection, and innovation, I won't be adding a bunch of delicate decorations. I want my children to be free to move, as toddlers do. Providing a minimalist "yes" space gives me more sanity.

SPACES FOR SCHOOL-AGE CHILDREN

Is your elementary-age child's space designed for studying, reading, creating art, resting, or something else? Let the answer determine how you design the space. It can be helpful to create a designated study area if your home allows. That might be the kitchen table, a homeschool room, or a desk in their bedroom.

SPACES FOR TWEENS AND TEENS

Is your teenager's space for privacy, hosting friends, or doing homework? Giving teens a secure and safe space where they can hang out and develop independence is good for the whole family. Design a space that reduces time spent in front of a screen and more time connecting with people.

Conclusion

Remember, minimalism in your home's living areas is not about stripping away everything—it's about giving yourself the space that will meet your needs without distracting you from your most important goals.

6 Kitchen

For many families, the kitchen is the heart of home. It's a place for cooking, eating, doing homework, and connecting with friends and family. A minimalist kitchen will help make all of these activities more enjoyable! Our kitchen sets the tone in our home. For this reason, it was one of the first common living areas I tackled at the start of my minimalist journey. My goal was to have a kitchen where I could de-stress, since so many stressful things happen there: meal preparation, snacks, homework, paper pileups, and schedule planning all take place in our kitchen.

First Steps to De-Clutter Your Kitchen

Before I talk about how to de-clutter your kitchen, let's review a few tips to help you be happy and successful with this challenge. These first steps are meant to preserve your momentum once you get going.

Remembering why you are de-cluttering is the fuel for your motivation. I do feel better when my kitchen is clean and well organized, but that is not my goal. De-cluttering my kitchen is about creating a place I want to cook in and where I find it easy and inviting to connect with family and friends.

Before you begin, bring your kitchen to its regular state of clean. Wash the dishes and put them away. Put away papers, keys, toys, backpacks, and mail. Designate a new home for each item so they don't end up on the counters or all stuffed into one drawer.

While it's tempting to think that we don't have enough space, more space isn't the answer to a minimalist kitchen. Just like more money coming in often leads to more money being spent, more space in our homes can easily lead to more stuff than we can happily manage. Rather than see physical boundaries as obstacles to overcome, I try to see them as friendly reminders of how much I can really manage. This is particularly true in your kitchen.

Will this be a slow and steady job tackling one cupboard at a time, or a relentless purge with every item on the chopping block? Feel free to break this project into smaller tasks. If you only have 15 minutes, plan for one cupboard or drawer. Definitely avoid pulling all the contents of a space out and running out of time to put away what you decide to keep.

As you de-clutter and find a home for what you're keeping, store each item in a place that makes it easy for you to use it. If you're not sure where that place is, make your best guess for now. Then pay attention to how you do particular tasks in the kitchen. Look at how practical, or not, it is to find and use what you keep. For example, keep your dishwashing liquid under the sink (where you use it). Practical placement in the kitchen equals sustainable habits. When we put things in odd places, we may be less likely to use them and even less likely to put them away. When you streamline your workflow, the change becomes welcome and more sustainable.

Clear Your Counters

I've often heard people say that horizontal surfaces are not their friend. It's easy to see why—they're more likely to collect a whole lot of things that are not useful and are distracting. Consider the tips below to clear and keep your counters open.

Until we set up a kitchen command center, a place for incoming everyday items like school papers, mail, and keys, our kitchen counters remained constantly cluttered. The command center lets our children know there is a designated spot for their belongings. We don't just set things down anywhere—everything has a home. In our home, our command center is in a kitchen cabinet. With fewer kitchen items, we have cupboard space to spare, so we don't have to have things out in the open. We have two trays to sort incoming papers and a basket for items like keys and wallets.

After setting up your command center to handle the flood of everyday items, you can properly implement a no-clutter guideline for your kitchen counters. Treat your kitchen counters like you treat your stove. Only put an item on it when you're doing something with it. Just as you wouldn't put papers on your stove, don't set papers on your counter. Adopt the perspective that placing—and keeping—items on your counter allows clutter-creep, and clutter-creep takes us in the wrong direction.

Many kitchen appliances are stored on the counter for convenience or because our cabinets are too full to hold them. Whenever possible, store your appliances out of sight. While you may think you don't want to get the toaster or coffeemaker out of a cabinet every morning, I encourage you to try it. You might enjoy having a clear counter for the remainder of your day more than you do the convenience of having the appliance available for one small task.

Keeping counters clear might feel like starting an exercise program—at first you dread doing the exercise, but you quickly discover that it really does make you feel better. It may be hard in the beginning, but once you've set up a space for those daily drop-off items (like keys, papers, and mail) and small appliances, keeping counters clear gets easier every day. The goal is to create a space that works for you and your family. When I keep my kitchen counters clutter-free I actually want to go into the kitchen and cook!

De-Clutter Your Cupboards and Drawers

If you're de-cluttering for the first time in your kitchen and feel overwhelmed, you could warm up to the task by tackling one drawer or one cupboard. After completing that space, de-clutter by category—pots and pans, glasses, utensils, silverware, and storage containers—until you have addressed everything in your kitchen. It's important to de-clutter by category because we often have similar items in different places. When we gather them, we can choose what to keep and then we'll know what we can let go of.

You'll also find your duplicates when you de-clutter by category; this is one reason why de-cluttering by category works so well! If you find two frying pans of similar sizes and realize you use only one, consider the other a duplicate and donate it.

As you gather the items from their cupboards and drawers, take this opportunity to wipe the cupboard or drawer clean. Next, evaluate each item and ask yourself some questions: How often do I use this item? Do I have another item that serves the same purpose? Is it still in good shape? Do I even like it? Consider the use-it-or-lose-it guideline for your kitchen items. Have you used this rice cooker or cheese grater in the last week, month, or year? If the answer is no, put it in the Give Away pile. Some items that commonly go unused are sandwich grills, fondue pots, ice cream makers, cappuccino makers, woks, sandwich presses, egg cookers, and bread machines. If you own one of these and use it often, then by all means keep it! At one point I had a KitchenAid mixer that I used every couple of weeks. Eventually, I couldn't justify keeping it when a hand mixer could complete the same task. It was pretty sitting on the counter, but when I looked at how often I used it, I couldn't see the value in keeping it.

Many small appliances today are not worth fixing if they are broken—sadly, it's often cheaper to replace them. I look for ways to do without small appliances—I make toast in our oven or fry bread in a pan if it's going to be a sandwich. My counter stays clear and I won't be throwing away a toaster. Before you replace the broken small appliance, look for a way to get the job done without it.

It is also important to keep in mind that another kitchen gadget is not necessarily going to make your life easier. For example: Consider ditching your apple cutter and using a knife. I thought our apple cutter was essential until I learned how to slice around the apple core with just four cuts from the top down. I also discovered I didn't need a garlic press when I learned how to crush and mince garlic with my everyday kitchen knife. Now I only wish I had learned that sooner. Ultimately, the most important items in your kitchen are the ones you use daily to prepare family meals.

Oftentimes our cupboards are overflowing with cups—sippy cups, plastic cups, coffee cups, cups with built-in straws. Consider keeping the quality cups and ditching the less durable ones. Keep fewer, multipurpose glass sets for your beverages. One way we did this was to use stemless wineglasses for wine and water. As you look at your glasses, think about whether can any be used for multiple beverages. If not, this is something to consider with future purchases.

Choose dishes that can be used for any occasion. Storing a second set of dishes takes up a lot of space for a little use. While I realize we all have different lifestyles, consider owning one dish set that can be used every day as well as for special occasions. I own the same white dish set my husband and I purchased when we got married and no one has ever seemed to enjoy their meal less because it wasn't served on fine china. But if you do have a second set of dishes that your family uses for special occasions and it brings you joy, keep it!

Another consideration is vases. I used to be a floral designer and had acquired many vases. I've pared my collection down to just a few I love the most. I enjoy having fresh cut greens and flowers in my home, so they get used often. I was able to purge all of my small- to medium-size vases without hesitation once I realized my glass canning jars were just as pretty.

Fix Your Food Storage

It is important to keep certain things in mind when applying minimalism strategies to your pantry. I always sort through my food and toss things past their expiration dates. As you go through your pantry, you could also try to get creative with the food that has been sitting there for a while. Grab a pen and paper and write down any ingredients you have, then use this list to help create meals.

I group my food into categories in order to reduce eye clutter. A few categories that I use are breakfast, snacks, and canned goods.

When I'm shopping for groceries I buy the items my family needs to eat for the week—not to fill my kitchen.

Clean Out Cookbooks

We find most of our recipes online these days. For years I held on to cookbooks that I inherited from my grandparents. My grandfather was Italian and made many wonderful meals from some of the recipes in these books. As time went on I found myself referring to them less and less. To simplify your cookbooks, set some guidelines that you feel comfortable with. Here are two guidelines that work for me.

* All cookbooks I keep must be used often and for multiple recipes. I want to use the things in my home. I don't keep cookbooks for decoration anymore. On a side note, it's okay to keep cookbooks that you rarely or never use but are sentimental items. Sort through them as sentimental items rather than as cookbooks.
* All cookbooks kept must provide more than five recipes I use. The number of recipes used will be determined by the size of your cookbook, but the idea is to not keep a cookbook for just a few recipes. This is how you end up with a bookshelf full of cookbooks taking up valuable space in your kitchen.

If the cookbooks you are sorting though have been in your possession and unused for more than six months, chances are that you're probably not going to get around to using their recipes. As you flip through the pages of your cookbooks, write down the page numbers of the recipes you want to keep. Consider scanning or photographing them and then printing them and putting them into a recipe binder where you can easily find them. Creating your own recipe binder is simple: use a three-ring binder and page protectors. You can also add binder tabs that separate categories.

If you want to reduce your paper and physical clutter altogether, consider keeping your recipes in a digital cookbook. You can add your scanned recipes to a PDF or create your cookbook with one of the many available online platforms. Simply search "create an online cookbook" to research the latest options. Although this does take a bit of time, consider how much time it can save you in the long run. Plus, your children and grandchildren will benefit from your one book filled with the recipes you actually use!

Conclusion

Clearing off your kitchen counters and cleaning out your cupboards and drawers will help you clear out your mind. Because it's often the heart of the home, the kitchen is a key component in creating a minimalist life.

7 Bedrooms

Our family has grown from two adults with one child to two adults with four children over the last ten years, and in this same time period we moved seven times. That's a lot of changes! Most of those moves also put us in temporary quarters for two to four weeks, managing several different sleeping arrangements each time.

As our family size increased and the moves continued, it was pretty clear to me that fewer possessions to unpack and arrange meant more time and energy doing what mattered more for us. The bedrooms were typically the first place we would start unpacking because having a place for restful sleep is important. All we cared about was getting our beds set up!

Your Bedroom

We all need rest, and most of us these days aren't getting enough. Lack of clutter and distractions are essential for adequate sleep. When you consistently sleep well, you have more positive energy to share with your family. De-cluttering your bedroom first, or very early on in your journey of becoming minimalist, can provide a place of calm as you sort through the rest of your home.

You may be tempted to de-clutter your child's bedroom first. Doing your own bedroom first is usually a smoother way to persuade your child to participate in de-cluttering their bedroom. You want them to see you enjoy the results of your minimalist bedroom. Getting better rest every night will also help you negotiate change with other members of your family.

Our bedrooms, like all other rooms in our home, serve a purpose. As you set out to de-clutter your bedroom, let that purpose help you determine what should stay and what should go. Most often our bedrooms are a place for rest and intimacy. Maybe your bedroom plays a dual purpose—such as an office, craft space, or reading nook. If it's necessary to make your bedroom a dual-use room, don't leave unfinished work where you can see it from your bed. Try to create visual barriers between where you go to sleep and where you do anything else.

Sometimes an unused bedroom can become a catchall for everything you're not sure what to do with. Sometimes our own bedroom is used to store this stuff. If de-cluttering your bedroom seems overwhelming, try the packing party method. (But if you're the only one packing, plan a simple reward for yourself such as resting with your favorite beverage after you've packed up some boxes.) Grab some boxes and pack up everything except the essentials you will need (like the linens on your bed). Mark a date on each box to remind yourself when to unpack and sort through them. Keep the boxes in a defined space, ideally out of sight of where you sleep, but where you can see them every day. The idea is to let you enjoy your bedroom as a place to rest.

If you're not using the packing party method, set up your Give Away, Put Away, Throw Away, and Not Sure boxes to collect the items you're removing when you're ready to start de-cluttering. Review the four-box method in the First Steps section of Chapter 2. Walk through the room and do a quick sweep, gathering items that you feel confident removing without hesitation. If you're feeling unmotivated and overwhelmed, set the timer for 10 minutes (or how-ever long you decide) and work until the timer goes off. Start with what feels like the easiest area of your bedroom for you.

FURNITURE

Too much furniture can be a distraction in itself. The pitfall with fur-niture is that it provides more places to collect clutter. If you need your dresser to store your clothing, keep the top simple and relaxing. You may not need a dresser if all of your clothing can be organized into your closet. You can also consider placing your dresser inside your closet if it fits well.

In our bedroom we have a bed, two night tables, a plant, and a small desk for my computer. We only recently moved the desk and computer into our bedroom as I've been writing more. With small children at home this is the best (and only!) place for me to write without interruption. (If you don't want to keep a night table, con-sider installing a simple wall shelf in its place. This will help you keep only your essentials at your bedside. With no drawers or second shelf there's less room for things to accumulate.) Since curating a minimalist bedroom, we've gotten rid of our armoire (and the TV inside it), a dresser (our wardrobes fit in our average American-sized closet), and a sitting bench. We haven't missed any of it!

DÉCOR

Have you ever thought about how simple and uncluttered a hotel room is? I don't think it's strictly to save money! A room with just enough decorations is refreshing and relaxing. As you sort through your bedroom, consider what you want there. Fresh linens, open space, your favorite tea on your night stand? Yes, please! Piles of clothes, stacks of papers, and odd furniture pieces? No, not so much! Be very selective and choose your favorite decorative pieces. Design your bedroom space for its intended purpose. Remove any item that does not directly support a feeling of rest, enjoyment, and relaxation.

CLOTHING

Just thinking about purging your wardrobe might be stressful and overwhelming. It requires forethought as well as the ability to let go of your past mistakes and your fantasy-self clothing. Success in simplifying your wardrobe (and life) is one part perspective change and one part finding the practical method to get you there. To get you thinking and get you started, I've compiled a list of perspective changes and practical methods to help you simplify and streamline your wardrobe.

1. **Avoid decision fatigue:** An exciting purchase becomes a burden when it's just one of too many choices of what to wear. Decision fatigue is not a good way to start the day. When we reduce our choices, we save our finite mental energy for things that matter more.

2. **Choose quality over quantity:** Owning 7 of the best T-shirts (in terms of fit, comfort, and style) is better than owning 20 good T-shirts.

3. **Say goodbye to comparison:** As you look in magazines and in stores for ideas and inspiration to build your capsule wardrobe (a simplified wardrobe that only contains items that you actually wear; see the box on page 93), take what works for you and leave the rest. Look through what you already have and enjoy wearing for items that are high-quality and versatile. Choose the fashion style that works for you and stick with it for as long as it continues working. In other words—if it works for you, don't replace it.

4. **Shop sales carefully:** Before you step into a sale, clearly identify your clothing needs. Know the fashion style that works best for you and define the number and type of clothing pieces you need. Ask yourself if you truly need a particular item and if would you buy it at full price. I'm all for taking advantage of sales if I actually need what is on sale.

5. **Realize it's perfectly okay to miss out**: Maybe a particular style is in right now and there are only a few pieces in stock. When you start to feel this kind of pressure, remind yourself of what matters more to you than fashion sales and trends. Corporations aren't going to remind you of that! When we choose to miss out, we're keeping room in our lives for more important things. Remember: You're not missing out, you're trading.

6. **Acknowledge when you can't let go yet:** Sometimes clothing is charged with emotion. The weight of holding on to it may be obscured by the emotional charge attached to it. Maybe the fact that it has sentimental value or belongs to your fantasy-self keeps you holding on. If you can't let go now, come back to it later. Keep moving forward where you can. You may find that the

practice of letting go of other items will make letting go of this one easier at another time.

7. **Practice generosity:** Other people may be able to benefit from the clothing you don't love and wear. It is better to give than to receive, and it is better to give than to keep what you do not need.

Having all of your clothing put away before you begin to de-clutter your wardrobe is an essential step in effectively sorting through it. If you live in a four-season climate zone, wait to see what favorites you actually use during each season before you purge. If you want to keep clothing pieces that need repair, plan to get the repair done ASAP.

With these perspectives in place, let's consider some popular practical methods for de-cluttering your wardrobe.

- **The Reverse Hanger Method:** The goal here is to make it easy to see which clothing pieces you use regularly. Place all of your hangers facing the same direction. After you've worn an item and put it back on its hanger, place the hanger on the rod in the opposite direction of all the other hangers. At the end of the season, you'll see exactly what you've worn and what you can donate.

- **The Last 14 Experiment:** Remove everything you have worn in the last two weeks from your drawers and closet. Box up the remaining items and put the box out of sight. Wait to see if you miss any of these items in the next 30 days. I'm embarrassed to say that when I did this years ago, I couldn't even remember some of the clothes I had in the box! This method has helped me simplify many areas of my home, including my bath and beauty products.

- **The Thankful Thread Challenge:** This is a challenge to give some of your clothes away to charities or shelters. It's a great way to de-clutter your wardrobe while growing your sense of gratitude. It has helped shift my kids' focus from having to giving. You can read more about it on my blog, *The Minimalist Plate*.

- **The LUK Method:** LUK means to Like, Use, and Know every item in your wardrobe (and home!). This approach comes from the philosophy I adopted at the start of our desire to live a more intentional life. For example, if you have three white shirts and only like one, keep the one. If you have three white shirts and only wear one, keep the one. If you have three white shirts and forgot about the other two, only keep the one. These anchor questions are easy for children to remember, and my kids easily applied this method to de-clutter their own wardrobes.

- **The Marie Kondo Method:** This is one of the most well-known methods for tackling clothing clutter. Gather every item of one kind, like jeans or T-shirts, into one big pile. Hold each item and ask, "Does this spark joy?" If your answer is no, thank the item and toss it in the goodbye pile.

Now that you've simplified your wardrobe, put away all of your items—each one should now have a proper place to live. You'll soon see the benefits of a de-cluttered wardrobe. After you've lived with it for a few weeks, you'll discover that it's easier and faster to find the clothes you want to wear and to focus on the style that you enjoy.

LINENS

Take out all of your linens and put them where you can sort through them. Recycle or repurpose damaged sheets and towels, or contact your local animal shelter to see if they can use them. Make a decision about how many items you need in each category: bath towels, beach towels, bedsheets, blankets, and others. For example, we have

A CAPSULE WARDROBE

A capsule wardrobe is a mini-wardrobe of essential and interchangeable clothing pieces. The upper limit of clothing pieces in a capsule wardrobe is typically fewer than 40. Before I started working on a capsule wardrobe, I was not particularly good at choosing clothes that worked best for my lifestyle and body. With time and effort, reducing my wardrobe gave me the clarity to define my personal style. Now, nearly every item of clothing I own reflects my style and is interchangeable. Having a simple collection of pieces that work well together means I'm not wasting time deciding if two items match—I now choose clothing that does! For example, I have a pair of gray jeans that can be dressed up with a silk top and heels or dressed down with a T-shirt and flip-flops. I also keep my accessories minimal and interchangeable with my wardrobe.

As I started thinning out my wardrobe, I picked out my favorite pieces to keep. I still ended up with clothing I didn't really love, because otherwise I wouldn't have had enough clothing to wear. I stuck with a minimal wardrobe and chose each new, needed item with careful consideration, and often only one piece at a time. My goal was to choose sustainable, comfortable, and affordable clothing in my chosen color palette. Building a capsule wardrobe helped me find better balance in my busy days.

eleven bath towels for our family of six. That breaks down to one towel per person, two guest towels, and three extras. I've found one beach towel per person is sufficient. We've kept two sets of sheets for our bed, six sets of sheets for our four kids' beds, and two extra mattress covers. If you feel like you need more than one set of extra sheets, ask yourself when they were used last. If they haven't been used in the last six months, chances are you can let them go. Storing each folded sheet set in its pillowcase is a good way to keep your linen closet well-organized.

Your Baby's Bedroom

Your baby's bedroom may be an easy room to start with or to take on right after finishing a more challenging room. You'll be making all the decisions, so simply tailor the de-cluttering tips from your bedroom—particularly regarding décor—to your baby's room, and combine them with the tips below. And remember, there's usually no shortage of people and places who will buy or accept used baby items in good condition.

FURNITURE

A safe sleeping place for your baby is essential. If you plan to have more children, investing in a solid crib that you can use for several years is a good idea. Otherwise you may want a crib that converts to a toddler bed to maximize the use of the furniture in your nursery. A comfortable place to change and dress your baby, as well as a comfy chair for soothing, should serve you and your baby well. If you are going to buy new furniture, choose a dresser and a chair that will work in an older child's room or another room later (especially since later, in this case, is not far off!).

Many parents may feel inclined to purchase an entire furniture set simply because the pieces go together. Be mindful of marketing techniques designed to make you feel like your baby's bedroom just won't be complete without a full set of furniture that includes items you don't need.

GEAR

In order to keep your home in a minimalist state, be sure to purchase baby gear only as needs arise. Also, donate or resell your quality baby gear after it's served your baby in order to avoid clutter-creep. We purchased a high chair from the resale market and sold it (in very good condition) three years later for nearly the same price. In the end, I think I paid $5 to use it for two children over a three-year period. Borrow baby gear (even for a day) whenever possible. I've been fortunate to have generous friends with children a little older than mine who were happy to lend me a sling or a baby carrier. Some essential gear we've used and resold or given away are: a stroller, travel crib, baby carrier, and bouncer. Check for safety recalls before you buy, donate, or sell baby gear and furniture.

CLOTHES

It can be risky completing your baby's wardrobe beyond their next growth spurt—they may not be able to or want to wear what you've purchased when they grow into it. For our family, 14 outfits of infant clothing for each child were enough. Maybe you'll need more, maybe you'll need less. Take into account how often you do laundry. If you wash clothing once a week, like I do, you'll need at least eight outfits to make it through the week. One outfit per day didn't cover diaper explosions and daily spit-ups in our home. I've read some minimalist baby clothing lists that recommend three to four newborn outfits during winter. The list writers are most likely doing laundry every day, or their child never gets their clothes dirty. My choice to do laundry once a week means having enough outfits for a week. Build a simplified wardrobe that aligns with other important choices in your life. If you plan to have more children in the near future and want to keep the baby clothing, define your storage space first (so you're less likely to keep more than you need or have space for) and keep only what is in excellent condition. Don't keep too much; remember that if your next child is born in a different season from the first child, the newborn clothes that you saved may not be appropriate for the weather. Also, avoid purchasing monogrammed items that can't be used again.

BOOKS

Have you ever noticed how young children can enjoy the same song, book, or show over and over again? We may be accustomed to lots of choices and new songs and stories, but that doesn't mean we need, or even thrive, with so many choices and changes. To de-clutter a baby's book collection, take out your favorites and donate the rest. We found that 8 to 15 books at a time was enough for our family. There are shelters and preschools in your local area that would be happy to receive your extra books.

CHILDHOOD KEEPSAKES

If you've been a parent for any length of time you know how quickly keepsake items can add up. Define a space for keepsakes as soon as possible. Limit the boundaries now, because expanding the boundaries later is easier than contracting them. It can be tempting to hold on to every keepsake item. But remember, we are the ones giving the value to our stuff. In our family, we have one box for each child and we add to it sparingly.

Your Young Child's Bedroom (Toddlers and Preschoolers)

Anytime is a good time to share the message of simplicity with our children, but the younger they are the easier it may be. There is never any guarantee that our children will embrace what we teach them—to build a purposeful life owning less stuff—but it's important to give them the tools and confidence for the journey. Here are the tips and strategies we used to help our three- and four-year-old boys de-clutter and embrace a minimalist mindset for their bedrooms. (Remember that the furniture and décor tips from your bedroom apply here as well.)

- **Everything has a home:** Every item in their room has a place. This idea can easily be turned into a game that builds a habit of knowing where to put and find things.
- **Be generous:** I believe that the greater power of generosity is its ability to motivate the giver to let go of lesser things. We talk to our children about giving some of their things up to others who can use them. I want my children to see giving as a way to pursue a greater purpose and more enduring joy.
- **Create a simple routine:** Simple routines are easier to establish and maintain when you're not distracted by clutter. Predictability builds trust and promotes calm in any household, but more so when you have children. With a simple routine, children can learn to internalize constructive habits and take charge of their activities.
- **Find simple storage:** Everything they play with is stored for function. I choose storage solutions that keep their toys accessible to them. My goal is to create a space that only occasionally needs

more than a little tidying up. Our kids can play and clean up more independently, and this reduces frustration for everyone.

- **Start a tradition of family cleanup time:** I much prefer maintenance cleanup than I do major cleanup routines. Every Saturday we do a quick family cleanup together. We each start with our own rooms. I may offer my children rewards (experiences instead of material goods) for helping their younger siblings after taking care of their own spaces. This routine helps minimize negative comparisons like "How come he isn't...?" or "Well, she's not..." and helps us maintain a rewarding habit of weekly maintenance.

TOYS

Moving frequently in the military with children has presented us with several storage arrangements. Sometimes we've stored toys in their bedrooms, and other times in a playroom or living room. Given the space, I always prefer to keep my young kids' toys out of their bedroom. I'm a big fan of rest and I'm a big fan of play, but I think that both are more enjoyable when the spaces for each are separated. Many parents try to de-clutter the toys first in their home when they start following a minimalist path. Sometimes it feels like they're everywhere—the kitchen, bedroom, bathroom, and always under your feet. But it can be helpful for your kids to have already watched you de-clutter much of your own stuff before you tackle theirs.

The optimum number of toys for any minimalist family will vary; ideally it stops short of too much. How do we know when we have too much? There is research that shows that young children actually play more when they have fewer toys! How is this possible? Children can't help but be distracted by their environment, and we allow the development of our children's creativity, imagination, initiative, and adaptability to be stunted when we overwhelm them with novel input. Fewer truly is better.

When choosing which types of toys to keep, consider ones that can be used in a variety of ways. We've found open-ended toys that can be used for varied ages and purposes most beneficial. Open-ended toys are generally toys that can't be completed or finished with quickly, like puzzles. A few examples of open-ended toys are art supplies, balls, sheets to build forts, and dolls for pretend play.

Next, narrow down the amount to keep in each category by choosing favorites. If your child has two number puzzles, keep one, or if your child has 10 stuffed animals, choose the favorite few. It's not so much about the number as it is about asking yourself if fewer will do the job.

Give everything a home and set limits for how big that home can be. This could be a shelf, drawer, or bin that all the toys must fit in. Allow your children to choose their favorite toys to keep in the designated space. Talk up a specific and relevant benefit for your young child—like more time to play at the park—when discussing toy limits. Offer an immediate reward that your child can do with you or another family member or friend after you've de-cluttered the toys.

I understand that some kids at this age may be very reluctant to part with any toys, never mind many of their toys. Try packing away several toys for two to three weeks and then give away what your child hasn't missed.

CLOTHES

All of my children have capsule wardrobes—and it's awesome! With less in their closets they can find and choose clothing that goes well together. Here are a few priorities in creating our kids' capsule wardrobes.

1. **Make a list:** We decided to keep roughly 10 outfits for each of our young children. While our 11-year-old daughter can wear her jeans a couple of times before washing, our boys' clothing needs to be washed after one wear. They love playing in the dirt! As you make your list, consider the specific needs for each child.

2. **Buy simple:** Oftentimes we purchase individual clothing pieces without taking into account versatility, and this easily leads to excess purchases. Instead, choose clothing pieces that are simple and versatile—they'll go with most anything in their closet. If you're purchasing an entire new wardrobe for your child, remember that it's easier to choose matching pieces if you shop from a small number of stores (or even just one).

3. **Buy comfortable:** It doesn't matter how great their clothes look if they aren't comfortable. When we wear things that aren't comfortable, we don't feel good in them—and that's what counts. I want our kids to be comfortable in their clothing. Plus, they're more likely to wear their clothes if they're comfortable.

Keeping a minimalist wardrobe for your young children can foster their independence and decision making. Consider storing outfits in easily accessible spaces for your child. As they learn how to dress themselves they can choose and access their clothing on their own. When we simplify our children's clothes, we simplify their daily life.

With three boys, we've found it helpful to keep one small container labeled by clothing size. As my kids outgrow their clothes, they can easily place these items in the container. You can also keep a container for donating items that don't work with their wardrobe.

ARTWORK

If you have children in school you know how quickly the artwork piles up: paintings, pottery, glitter art, painted T-shirts for every occasion, and paper with uncooked noodles glued to them. I enjoy seeing the things my children have created. But that doesn't mean I have to hold on to everything they've ever made.

At the same time, it may be difficult to let it go. The artwork is a gift from your child. Your child is most likely proud of their artwork and it may hold emotional value. But keeping every work we create is not a good or healthy option for our family. As a result, we've set some boundaries. We are always sharing with our children the fact that we can place the value in the experience, the thought, and the memory, not necessarily the thing. To control the artwork in our house, we created an art wall in our toddlers' bedroom with a wire cable and clips to display their most recent or favorite artwork. When this space is full and they create new artwork to display, another one must come down to make room for it. (If you want to keep a record of the artwork you could digitize it before getting rid of it.) As we tuck them into bed each night they can see and have time to enjoy their creations. It brings me joy to hear my three-year-old say, "Look, Mommy, that's the kite I made for you and Daddy." I love how happy my children are about the simple and beautiful things they've created.

BOOKS

If you want your children to enjoy the books they have—give them fewer. See how your child does with about 10 to 15 favorite books at home. Put them where your child can easily retrieve and return them. If they are constantly throwing and leaving books on the floor, work on crafting a routine to take care of them. A local library is a wonderful resource. You can connect with real, live people in your community, read as much as you like for free, and enjoy fun learning activities designed for all ages.

Your School-Age Child's Bedroom

While toddlers and preschoolers need constant supervision, school-age children gradually become ready for more independence. They are learning to make good choices on their own, be a kind friend, and exercise self-discipline. Implementing minimalism in your child's life is a gift in keeping with the things that matter most. If you are just starting out becoming minimalist with your kids, it's important to remember that becoming minimalist is just as much about a perspective change as it is about de-cluttering things from your life. It takes time to shift our thinking and embrace new beliefs. If your kids aren't jumping for joy to toss their excess, remember that they need time to shift their thinking, too.

Our school-age children are responsible for managing their possessions in their bedrooms. We work together to help them define the spaces where they will keep their belongings (using, in part, the furniture and décor tips from our bedroom, adapted to their ages). We let them know it's their responsibility to maintain some sense of order and cleanliness. We do not expect perfection, but we also don't want to step on or over things when tucking them into bed.

Rather than being continually drawn to the next new toy or gadget, we want our children to play with and enjoy what they already have, and we want them to learn to choose well what to spend themselves on. When our children want to spend their own money on another possession, we talk about what they will have to do to take care of it, whether or not there is something else they might enjoy more, and how long they think this item might last. Even though they may have no real answers at first, we still want to instill in them a habit of asking these questions so they can learn how to answer them.

One of our sons (who was around six years old at the time) was given a talking Spider-Man action figure, and he was certain he would love it forever. But after two days he stopped playing with it. A few months later he wanted to purchase a cool new talking toy. I gently asked him about the action figure—the one he hadn't touched for months. I suggested to him that this new toy wouldn't seem cool either after two days, just like Spider-Man. I asked him to think about the decision to get this toy for a bit and he agreed. A few days later he decided entirely on his own not to get it. It's easier to let go of things—all kinds of things—when we can examine our mistakes without fear and blaming.

TOYS

With my school-age children I try to choose toys that can be used for different play activities. Magna-tiles are a favorite open-ended toy in our home. The idea is to encourage your child to spend most of their time exploring what they can do with a toy. Too many toys distract a child from this kind of exploration. Instead, the child moves more quickly from one toy to the next toy, asking only "What is this?" not "What can I do with this?"

You can still make parting with toys fun for your child in their elementary years. Look for shelters or charities that will accept donations. Give your child an opportunity to choose the recipient. Have a yard sale and let your child keep the earnings from their excess. If your yard sale efforts don't yield much of a return, explain how this is a valuable lesson in resources. It takes time and energy to part with things, so let's set ourselves up to do this as infrequently as possible.

If you find your children are reluctant to part with their excess toys, ask them to participate in an experiment. You pack up a box of toys and then your child goes in to their bedroom to see if they can identify what's missing. This experiment is not to take their toys away but to show them that if they can't remember what they own, maybe they have too much stuff, or maybe their stuff isn't really all that cherished.

CLOTHES

Work with your child to decide the size of their wardrobe and how to make it a capsule wardrobe. Our eight-year-old son's summer wardrobe has roughly nine pairs of shorts, nine tops, two bathing suits, and four pairs of shoes. We got to this size after he identified his favorites. I selected a couple more outfits for special occasions and a spare outfit. After working together to choose the clothes, my son was happy to donate the rest. If your child doesn't want to let go of the excess, or you aren't convinced you won't need these items, pack them away with an expiration date. When the date arrives, reassess your family's need for the items. Meanwhile, let your child see you donate your excess, and look for more opportunities to show him the benefits of letting go of what is too much for us to use and care for.

Look back to the tips for creating a kid's capsule wardrobe on page 100. In short: Make a list, buy simple, and buy comfortable.

SCHOOL PAPERS

Oh, the papers! Our children—from preschool through elementary grades—bring a tidal wave of papers home every week. I value parent-school communication but prefer a digital format. To get the school papers under control we use our command center in the kitchen. This is our designated area for school papers. I sort papers from there into a folder to scan and file (like progress reports) or into a current tasks tray (to sign and send back, or events to consider attending). I also take photos and add events to my calendar immediately so I can recycle the paper. If your child is in the habit of stashing papers in their room, help them choose a spot to keep them. Think about giving your child a folder, a drawer, or a tray for this purpose. When it starts to overflow, let them know it's time to cull through it.

ARTWORK

When our kids bring home art that they love and are most proud of, it's important that their masterpiece be noticed and appreciated. To honor their excitement and joy we display it for a period of time. With uncluttered rooms, our kids' most often display their favorite artwork in their bedrooms. After a period of time they or I suggest that we recycle it or take a photo of it. If they feel it's really amazing they'll keep it in a folder and refer back to it over the next year. As our children have grown in our minimalist lifestyle, they've become more apt to look back after some months or a year and let it go.

BOOKS

Too many books can present a problem in a minimalist household, just like too many toys. There's good reason to maintain a curated library of books, rather than adding unlimited books to a child's collection. Remember that children benefit from re-reading books. Re-reading helps them develop their comprehension and vocabulary. Encourage your children to ask questions about the story they've read and give them plenty of opportunities to use the words they learned in the story. (This helps them learn how to learn and learn how to engage with other people.) The value of books is not found in how many you own.

If your child is in elementary school, chances are that you're familiar with book fairs. While there are some excellent books offered, there are also knickknacks, toys, and books with movie and product tie-ins. Help your child make thoughtful use of book fairs rather than getting caught up in the excitement. I ask our children a few gentle questions to help them make thoughtful choices at the book fair like, "Do you have room on your shelf for new books?" and "Can the book you want be borrowed from the library?" Take this opportunity to teach your child about conscious consumerism. We don't have to buy things (even books!) just because there is a book fair and our friends are buying stuff, too. Anything you don't need on sale is still something you don't need.

Encourage your children to borrow books from the library (be sure to get them a library card as soon as they can sign their name) or consider buying books for an e-reader. Digital books are typically cheaper than their paperback or hardcover counterparts, and they take up much less space!

Once you've helped your children de-clutter their books, be sure to donate them to places that could use them: schools, hospitals, shelters, and libraries.

COLLECTIONS

Kids and their collections . . . Like all trends, they fade and typically so does our child's desire to keep them. If you already have an oversized collection to contend with, work in measured steps. Keep the collection in its designated space and use the one-in-one-out rule, be an example with your own possessions, highlight the benefits of owning less stuff, and help your children manage their other possessions before taking on the collectibles. The danger with collections is that the goal is simply to collect. It's a more, more, more mindset. Defining the maximum space for our kids' things has kept their collections in check.

Your Teenager's Bedroom

If de-cluttering and living in a more minimalist way is new to your teen, you may need to ramp up the persuasion. Teenagers thrive on independence but crave reassurance—so walking this path with diplomacy will go a long way! It's important to take into account the challenges of the simplicity message reaching teens specifically. Teenagers, like many adults, place their value and worth in the things they own and the clothes they wear. Advertisers target their message to teens well—and they spend billions and billions of dollars doing it.

Before you suggest that your teen de-clutter their bedroom, remind them that the freedoms that teenagers often desire—financial freedom, freedom to spend time with friends, and the freedom to pursue a greater purpose—are more attainable with a minimalist lifestyle.

If your teen has no interest in purging their bedroom clutter, suggest de-cluttering one space in their bedroom at a time. Maybe they're willing to simplify their wardrobe or a study area in their room. Offering to help might be a way to let your child know you're on their team. It's also possible that your teenager may respond better to a challenge to do this independently. You know your teen and how best to motivate them. Gaining more floor space for desired activities and hobbies might provide an additional motivation to create a clutter-free, organized space.

FURNITURE

Encourage your teen to minimize horizontal surfaces. Suggest they get rid of extra bookshelves and tables if all they do is collect clutter. If it's in your family budget, offer them one piece of useful furniture they'd love as a reward after they've cleared the clutter from their room. This will help them see the potential and value of their space.

DÉCOR

Teens are more likely than younger children to decorate their rooms themselves. If possible, offer to help them clear the décor completely and reintroduce just their favorite key pieces. Let your teen decide what decorations, artwork, and memorabilia to keep, but let them know that you aren't planning on holding everything for them when they leave for college. In other words, it's going to be their responsibility to take it with them if they want to keep it. This may help cut down on decorative clutter!

CLOTHES

Your teen may care a great deal about wearing the latest trends. Reassure your children that their value lies in their character—not in what brand of clothing they wear. You may also want to share the environmental impact and social justice issues around our culture's excessive clothing consumption as additional motivation to de-clutter.

In practical terms, define the space that your teenager's wardrobe may occupy. Should everything fit in the dresser and the closet (and not on the floor or in the coat closet)? Use the same de-cluttering tips for your teen's wardrobe that you've used for yourself, and be sure to pass them along to your teen, who may want to de-clutter without your help. Let them know what the options are for getting rid of excess clothes. If your teen has a pile of "not sure" clothing, help them pack it away with an expiration date. Revisit the items when the expiration date arrives. Ask your teen if they can gift the items they didn't need. What happens if they won't limit their wardrobe or get rid of clothes they rarely (or never) wear? Don't do their laundry at all, or only if certain conditions are met, if you believe they need more experience with the ongoing cost of owning clothes.

Limit your contribution to their wardrobe to essentials that fit within a capsule wardrobe. As with an adult wardrobe, the key to building a minimalist wardrobe for a teen is versatility. How many pieces can one clothing item be matched with? The more, the better! Avoid buying clothing that can be worn only on specific occasions or in certain weather conditions. Shop with your teenager and help them choose items that can be mixed and matched. If your teen is willing, give them a challenge: See if they can estimate how many outfits one new piece of clothing can make with what they already own. Again, don't buy things for them that they don't need.

SCHOOL SUPPLIES AND PAPERS

Teenagers need backpacks, notebooks, binders and dividers, folders, planners, loose-leaf paper, graph paper, and pens, pencils, and high-lighters for school. Some ways to cut down on the number of items in this list include using a multi-pocket folder instead of individual folders for each class, a multi-subject notebook, and composition notebooks or a legal pad instead of loose-leaf paper. Digitizing as much as possible will reduce a lot of the paper clutter they bring home. They may want or need to keep some of their school papers; give them a storage space specifically for this purpose so that their papers don't end up all over your house.

BOOKS

As with younger children, encourage your teens to use the library and consider reading digitally. They will probably know all the digital options already!

Remind your teen that books can be profitable if sold online. If your teen has stacks of books they're holding on to and not using, encourage them to donate them or sell them online. Let them keep the profits. Remind them that they will continue to acquire books now and when they go to college, so they'll want to stay on top of their growing collection and keep it in check. Their bedroom is not a storage unit.

Conclusion

Bedrooms can be tough to de-clutter and tough to maintain, but with a minimalist mindset and the tips and strategies above, all family members can help keep their spaces clutter-free.

8 Home Office

Whether your home office is its own room or part of another room, keeping it clutter-free and organized is essential for productive work. An office in its own room that has available horizontal surfaces can function more as a clutter magnet than an office if you are not conscious of it. While I'm not suggesting you give up easy access and doors for privacy, I am suggesting you consider giving up extra horizontal surface area so you can reclaim your office as a place for productive work.

The first thing to do with an office that has turned into a clutter magnet is to take out everything that doesn't facilitate productive work for you. Take out trash and recyclables, and then anything else that is unrelated to your work. If it isn't helping you in the purpose of doing your work, it doesn't belong. Sort what's left on your desk. If you're using the four-box method to handle the flow of items in your office, consider adding a shred pile. But be sure to put it in its own box for another time.

Rethink Office Basics

Although an office or an office space includes some of the same elements as other living spaces, it also has elements that make it unique. Here are issues specific to offices to consider when living a minimalist lifestyle.

FURNITURE

What is the purpose of your office? Is it for you to work from home? For your children to study in? Or does it have another purpose? Choose the essential pieces of furniture that help you accomplish your purpose. I give space in my office only to what adds value—for me, that's a small desk, a computer chair, and a plant. I keep the space around these items clear so I can move around with ease. If your desk has more horizontal space than you need to get your work done, you might consider replacing it with a smaller one when the time is right. For now, you can use it to sort through excess papers. When you've finished this task, note how good it feels to have that clear space!

ELECTRONICS

What electronics are essential to you and your home office? Separate those and box up the rest. If you haven't used particular pieces over the course of a month, consider recycling or donating them. See page 69 for places to recycle and donate electronics.

Do you have electronics that serve only one purpose when they could serve two or more? Previously we had a scanner and a printer.

Now we have a wireless printer-scanner-copier and lots more free space.

When I began asking myself questions about my electronic possessions, I found I didn't really use or need many of them. Along with getting rid of what I don't need, I've embraced learning how to use electronics differently and more efficiently.

OFFICE SUPPLIES

As you sort through your office supplies, you'll find that the easiest place to start reducing is with duplicates. When I began simplifying my office supplies I found four staplers, three hole punchers, five pairs of scissors, and three dozen pens. Limit your extra supplies. The little stuff is just the kind of stuff that sneaks up on you. Donate your excess supplies to local schools in need.

MAIL

Some weeks, junk mail was the only mail we got. I was disturbed at the paper waste and clutter that it created. You can stop junk mail by contacting the sources of your junk mail and requesting to be removed from their mailing lists. You can call credit card, insurance, and catalog companies directly for the same reason. If you prefer doing this task online, here are a few places to start.

- To cancel credit card and insurance offers, visit OptOutPrescreen.com
- To cancel direct mail, visit DMAchoice.org
- To cancel catalogs, visit catalogchoice.org

It is easier than ever to switch from paper to electronic billing. You can receive nearly all of your bills electronically and then pay them online. If you're not doing this already and you'd like to, look at your paper bills for information about how to do this. Don't forget that you can move your banking online, too, thereby eliminating statements and other paper clutter.

Even after requesting to be removed from a company's mailing list, you may still receive junk mail from other companies. Designate a place for the junk mail to go. Keep trash and recycling bins (and perhaps a shredder) nearby so that you can dispense with the mail quickly.

PAPERS

Most often we struggle with paper clutter because we lack the habits needed to keep our papers organized and simplified. I need to organize and simplify my papers in order to get my office work done and be able to easily find specific papers when I need them.

The most important principle for organizing your papers is that everything must have a home. Make sure you have a place for each category of paper you keep: receipts, bills, insurance, tax returns, and so on. It may be helpful to divide your financial papers into categories: tax records, papers to keep for the calendar year or less, and papers to keep indefinitely. (People often ask how long should they keep their tax returns and tax-related records, and I always recommend they visit IRS.gov for the latest information. We keep one paper copy of last year's tax returns to help in preparing next year's tax returns.) Put your papers away as soon as possible in order to keep clutter at bay.

Even digital files need a home if you hope to find them again, so remember that you also need to put digital files where you can find them. Divide them into categories just as you did with your papers.

If you keep documents in both digital and hardcopy formats, you're paying for duplicate storage. Digital space costs money, as does paper, folders, a filing cabinet, a shredder, a printer, and ink. You're also paying more in terms of your time and energy for duplicate storage.

Many statements these days can be retrieved online for at least several months, so you don't need to keep things like utility bills (to prove residency, for instance). You can download them when you need them. Simplify your record keeping by signing up for electronic statements from all of the creditors and financial institutions you use.

Set aside time each week to go through your papers. (We do this on Saturday mornings.) Regular maintenance will keep the clutter at bay and prevent you from sorting through the same papers twice (or more).

Digitize Your Office

There are many things in your office that can be digitized, saving you space and time in the long run. Scan the physical photos that are collecting dust on your desk. If you don't have a scanner, office supply stores often have services to suit your scanning needs. Consider letting go of the DVD collection that's cluttering up the bookshelf in your office. With technology today, you can rent virtually any movie instantly. Ditch your CDs, too. Transfer your music to your computer and use a cloud-based software like iCloud or Dropbox to store it.

As noted earlier, you can set up online accounts for all bills and receive your statements via e-mail. In doing so you will reduce incoming paper bills and the need for envelopes and stamps to send the bills; you'll also free up time you would have spent sorting bills and the space they would have occupied on your desk.

If you have magazine subscriptions, choose electronic versions over paper versions. The magazines won't create clutter on your desk and you'll be less likely to let them hang around for a long time.

Do you tend to keep user manuals (for your vacuum, dishwasher, dryer, and so on) in your office? Now is the time to get rid of them. Take a photo of the top page for reference and store it on your computer in your "manuals" folder. If you need the manual's specific information, refer to the model number in your photo and find the manual online.

Start using notes on your smartphone or computer. Once you've digitized your notepads and stickies you'll be able to let go of extra notepads, sticky pads, and other paper pads, as well as extra pens and pencils. If you must have a physical way to take notes, consider having one bullet journal.

De-Clutter Your Digital Space

Going digital is a great way to reduce your office clutter—but you don't want to simply trade physical clutter for digital clutter. It's important to remember that the most effective way to be and stay organized is to keep a whole lot less!

As with your physical papers and projects, create a home for everything and set aside time once a week or so to keep your papers and projects organized.

YOUR COMPUTER DESKTOP

It's convenient to save things to your desktop and leave them there. Treat your desktop like you treat the top of your physical desk or your kitchen counters—cleared! A tidy looking desktop is just as satisfying as a tidy office space, and a lot easier to maintain. Create a temporary or to-do folder just as you would for your work space. Oftentimes it's all too easy to treat our computer desktop like a dumping ground. At the end of each day (or week) clean out your desktop folders and discard anything you don't need.

PHOTOGRAPHS

This is one area in which I still need to de-clutter. I've made two passes through my digital photos but still want to simplify a bit more. It's easy to get carried away with digital photos when you love taking pictures of your kids! Apply the same principles from your paper photos to your digital photos. And back them up!

DE-CLUTTER YOUR E-MAIL

Unsubscribe from every e-mail list that isn't adding value to your life. For the next few weeks, handle every unwanted e-mail as soon as you see it. E-mails sit in our inbox because we simply haven't made a decision. Give every message you want to keep a home. Set up folders and tell your e-mails where they need to go.

I used to keep e-mails sitting in my inbox to remind me of events, dates, or projects I wanted to attend. Adding them to my monthly calendar has been a better way to remind myself and keep the clutter at bay.

Conclusion

Whether creating open space in your office (or on a table in the corner that serves as your office) or freeing up your digital space, minimalist principles play an important role in helping you concentrate on what you value most.

9 Bathroom

De-cluttering your bathroom can be one of the best places to start your minimalist journey. It's usually one of the smallest rooms in your home and has very few, if any, sentimental items. The single technique that helped me to significantly simplify my beauty and bath products was experimenting by elimination. I removed about 80 percent of my beauty products for two weeks. This allowed me to live with less immediately without having to make the decision to get rid of it right away. After a couple of weeks I found I didn't need many of the products I had. In fact, I couldn't even remember some of them!

Many of us already suspect that we have too many products in our bathroom. Yet we continue to pack our medicine cabinets. Why? We love having choices and hate to miss out on something good. For example, you may have several different kinds of hair and skin care products. Unfortunately, this can leave your bathroom storage spaces jam-packed with "extras" to last you through the next two years. By then, half of them will have expired and the other half will no longer interest us—because we've been out shopping for something better.

Remember that you don't need one specialty product for every possible hair and skin care need for each member of your family. Look for multipurpose products that multiple members of your family can use.

De-Clutter Your Bathroom

To start, empty all the movable contents from your medicine cabinet and vanity. When you start pulling everything out you'll find that the little stuff really does add up. Sort through your bath and beauty care products and put back only what you've used in the last week. If you're feeling bold, try a different strategy: If you haven't touched a product at least every other day, don't place it back in. You can keep essential items needed for special events in a separate container— they don't need to be stored in your everyday collection—and put the container under your bathroom sink or in a nearby de-cluttered closet.

After you have sorted, be sure to keep the items you use regularly out of sight as much as possible. If your products live on your counter because your bathroom doesn't have any storage, try finding a simple storage cabinet you can hang on the wall to hold the essentials. If that's not possible, consider a small free-standing storage cabinet. Keep any visible horizontal space in your bathroom cleared. The sight of cleared surfaces can help you relax.

What about the products you don't use daily or keep for special occasions? As you sort through this pile of products, remove the duplicates and the unnecessary items. If you have enough shampoo to last for the next five years, you could donate some to a local shelter. Pare down your grooming products, too: hair brushes, nail clippers and files, and so on. Much of what you're left with can be tossed, donated, or kept packed away until you're confident you can live without it.

Another thing to keep in mind is medicine. Your kitchen will likely provide a drier environment for medication than the bathroom and may offer more storage options. (Just be sure to keep the medicine away from heat.) Wherever you decide to store medication, ask if it will be accessible to the person who takes it, and be sure to keep it safely away from those who shouldn't have access to it. When de-cluttering, check all expiration dates and toss what's no longer viable. Be sure to follow local guidelines for disposing of unwanted medication.

Consider the Décor

The goal with bathroom décor is to create a simple, clean space that helps you relax. Your bathroom is probably one of the smallest rooms in your home, so any extra décor is likely to make it feel cluttered. Pick a few decorative items that help you feel calm. How many that few is will depend on how much space you're working with. If you're unsure, go with less than you think you need. Wait a week or more to see how it works for you.

Make Your Bathroom Kid-Friendly

De-cluttering your child's bathroom or de-cluttering your child's belongings in the family bathroom will provide them with only what they need and nothing else to distract them. Once we simplified our kids' bathroom they had less stuff to get into and—best of all—our elementary-age kids can now clean it entirely on their own.

To help teens de-clutter, show them how to follow the experimenting-by-elimination steps above. This can be a great learning experience that shows them how much stuff they've been keeping in general that they really don't use.

Currently my young kids keep the following items in their bathroom:

- Toothbrush
- Toothpaste
- Dental floss
- Hairbrush
- Hair and body bar soap
- Toilet paper
- Towels
- Humidifier (for when they're sick)
- Two paintings (gifts from a talented and kind neighbor)

While these limited items work for young kids, teens may need different items or more items. Just be sure to keep the bathroom possessions in check.

Conclusion

Bathrooms are relatively easy spaces to de-clutter due to their size. But remember that the number of items is not the end goal; reducing your excess so you can spend more time on what matters is.

10 Basements, Attics, and Other Storage Spaces

We cherish things and we accumulate them. We move them from room to room, room to basement, room to garage, and room to attic. And one out of ten Americans rents off-site storage to store more things. MJ Rosenthal, a professional organizer, says the average American home contains 300,000 items, from salad forks to sofas. And I'm wondering, does this number reflect the things we're keeping in our basements, attics, and garages? Either way, what in the world are we doing with 300,000 items in our home?

These storage spaces—whether they are your basement, attic, or another area—can be the most difficult spaces to simplify. Maybe we see ourselves as invested in all of this stuff, maybe we like keeping the option of making good use of it later, maybe we feel overwhelmed just thinking about sorting through and making decisions about it. Sometimes these spaces cause so much stress that we simply want to shut the door and pretend our stuff isn't even there.

Whatever the reasons, keeping all of this stuff prevents us from living our better lives. We need to spend some of our physical and emotional energy on these clutter-dump areas in order to be free to define our lives in more meaningful ways as we move forward.

Holiday Decorations

For many families, decorating for the holidays has become a time-consuming and expensive undertaking. While I personally enjoy holiday decorations, we can often get carried away turning a joyful event into a stressful season. Decorations for each individual holiday take work to maintain and require storage space in our homes. But I believe it is entirely possible to buy less and decorate less and still have a happy, joyful, and beautiful holiday. Hopefully the decorations are just an accessory to the celebration of your holiday. When we keep things simple we leave room for the things we value most.

Along the way I realized I don't have to do things the way they've always been done—and you don't have to, either. You don't have to use and keep all of the decorations you've been given. And you don't have to decorate the way you've always done it in the past. Focus on the purpose, experiences, and the values you want to create for your family. Now, how many boxes of holiday decorations do you need to do this? Only you can decide that.

While I personally feel there is value in sharing ideas through photos, the success of my child's birthday party does not depend on its Pinterest worthiness. It's easy to get hung up on picture-perfect parties. But I want to celebrate the life of my child, and I do this best when I keep things simple. One way we've kept decorations simple for our four kids' birthday celebrations is to have one happy birthday banner (made from felt) that we use every year for all of them. We hang it on the wall and let our child take center stage. No need to spend time purchasing party decorations that will end up in a landfill year after year.

Holiday decorations have meaning because we gave that meaning to the decorations. We can take it back and put it someplace better. We can choose fewer items and spend more of ourselves connecting with family and friends in our celebrations.

De-owning holiday decorations might be easier in the month or so preceding the holiday because the holiday is on your mind, but that's not to say it shouldn't be done at any other time. Our Christmas decorations once filled four large storage bins. We de-cluttered those bins throughout the year, and now we're down to one bin. It holds stockings, tree lights, ornaments, and a few sentimental decorations. We no longer store wrapping paper, tissue and ribbons; we use brown paper bags that our children decorate for wrapping our gifts. We don't keep an artificial tree. I enjoy bringing in fresh cut greens or flowers to decorate for each holiday; I love the natural feel living things bring to a room. Plus, I don't have to store a tree during the year.

Sports Equipment

I often hear people say, "It's hard to keep kids' sports equipment organized with all the different activities they're in." And to that I might ask, "Is it possible they're involved in too many sports activities?" I'm a huge fan of under-scheduling, in keeping with a minimalist lifestyle.

Kids have different sports for different seasons and unlike adults, kids grow out of their sports equipment fast! A swap or resale program for youth sports equipment may be available in your community. If not, maybe you could organize one.

Sports equipment often ends up being stored in different areas of the home—in our kids' closets, under their beds, or in the entryway, garage, or the trunk of our car. I'm always on the lookout for randomly stored assorted balls, sport-specific shoes, racquets, weights, climbing or camping gear, kettle bells, and hockey sticks. Gather all the equipment up and assess what you have versus what you need. Keep similar categories together. Define a space for everything. Wall mounted racks can be a good way to keep clutter off the floor.

As you sort through your family's sports equipment, ask yourself some questions. Does my child still want to play this sport? Are these shoes really going to fit my child next season? Take note of the equipment you know you'll have to buy new so you can let go of these items as soon as they don't fit.

Look at your own sports equipment, too. Has your tennis racquet sat on a shelf for the past year? How many times have you actually used your treadmill? Is it part of your fantasy-self?

Sports equipment is typically designed for a specific purpose, so repurposing it requires creativity and time that you may not have. Sports equipment can't be recycled. Extend its useful life as much as possible by swapping, sharing, reselling, or donating it before sending it out with the trash.

Craft Supplies

Taking advantage of sales and stocking up on supplies we won't be using in the near future isn't always the good deal we think it is. We typically don't consider the full cost in getting caught up in catching good deals. We also forget that our artistic eye may change, moving from one trending item to the next. If you have a craft as a hobby, keep only what you need to finish one or two current projects. Finish one project at a time and don't buy more supplies for projects until then. Even if they're on sale! Accumulating too many supplies typically ends up taking valuable time, energy, and resources away from actually creating.

Define the space you will use to give a home to all of your supplies. Be mindful of how well you can manage all of the designated space and categories you assign to it. My goal is to not let keeping supplies on hand interfere with, or compete with, actually enjoying my chosen craft. I don't want to live as if getting the most craft supplies for the best price is in and of itself what I enjoy.

You might ask yourself: How much material do I need to make three months' worth of projects? How many pieces of canvas or watercolor paper will I use in the next six months? Be ruthless and honest with yourself about how much you will use in the near future. Don't let craft clutter put a damper on your creativity.

Tools

Just the nature of the word *tools* makes all tools sound useful, so maybe it's easy to think that more really is better with them. But the minimalist principles don't change. Know what you need in order to do the jobs you realistically expect you will do. To sort out the essentials, first create a group of tools to go into a basic toolbox. Our family toolbox includes a screwdriver set, a hammer, pliers, an adjustable wrench, a utility knife, a level, a tape measure, a flashlight, a hacksaw, and an electric drill. Any duplicate items you come across while sorting can be sold or donated. Next, define a space for those needed tools that don't belong in the basic toolbox. If your tools have been living on the ground, consider putting them in simple wall storage cabinets. Keep items out of sight as much as possible. Renting or borrowing may be a better option than storing a pricey tool for occasional use. Consider that it is indeed possible to have too many tools. After all, what good is a tool that never has the chance to be used?

Garden and Yard Equipment

Investing in minimal wall storage for your garden and yard equipment can free up floor space in your garage. Don't keep extra garden hoses, watering cans, grills (when's the last time you used that portable grill?), flowerpots, or old garden furniture. When the watering can you're using finally bites the dust, you can replace it with a new one—or even use a pitcher from your kitchen. If you keep broken or habitually empty pots, give yourself some peace and get rid of them. Leaving them there serves only as a reminder that you killed the last plant living in it. We often hold on to other yard items that are broken, thinking that we'll fix them. If you have equipment in your yard or garage that is broken or an eyesore, schedule a pickup to have it hauled off.

Conclusion

You can keep your big storage spaces clutter-free by using general minimalist principles and the specific tips above. Keeping them free will keep you free!

Part Four

Maintenance: The Benefits of Less

Congratulations on coming this far! If you haven't made as much progress as you had hoped by now, don't worry. I think that's the case for most of us. I encourage you to continue along, using the strategies you've learned.

Now it's time to learn to keep the space clear that you've already de-cluttered. As you continue on this path, minimalism will become a natural rhythm in your life. Maintaining minimalism in your home may not feel quite as exciting as it initially did, and the changes you make now might not be as significant as the first changes you made, but that may be just what you're after!

Achieving minimalism with your possessions is just the beginning. Now you have the time, space, and energy to get excited about things that matter more, like your passion and purpose. While removing our excess stuff is where we started, we need to do what it takes to keep the clutter out in order to enjoy our newly found freedom. The hard work that you have done will make maintaining the simple space easier. It can be challenging, though, to keep the stream of stuff out of your home when you have kids or a partner who continue to bring more in, or family members who keep on giving. Here's what to do.

11 Keeping It Clean

Becoming minimalist is a process, one typically done in steps. You've already taken many of those steps. The best way to prevent a relapse is to enjoy the space and time you've reclaimed, because minimalism is not about denial! This enjoyment will motivate you to keep the distractions from returning. Some will sneak in, but you'll be prepared to deal with them.

Short-Term Solutions

Routines can help you and your family develop new habits to keep your home clutter-free. Here are some routines and helpful ways for you and your family members to work together to keep the clutter out.

REVIEW HOUSE GUIDELINES

Sometimes as we're using a particular room, we talk with our children about how well our guidelines are being followed, and let them know we're open to changing the guidelines if we can agree on a good reason to do so. This lets us review our minimalist guidelines with them while at the same time giving them lots of opportunities to meet challenges and think critically.

PARE DOWN AGAIN IN STAGES

The need to continue de-owning after the initial clearing out is not unusual. You probably have items that you owned when you began your journey and have recently decided they no longer add value to your life. And you may have acquired some items since you began that you now believe you don't need. This is perfectly okay. There's no shame in needing to continue to part with things that no longer serve your purpose. As you and your family members grow into minimalism, continue assessing what serves this current season of your life. De-owning is one of the quickest and best ways to free up your time so you can live a minimalist lifestyle.

DEFINE A SPACE FOR WHAT WILL GO OUT

Designate a box in a common area of your home where family members can place things they no longer need. Decide if this box is for donating or selling items. If you're not getting rid of an item right away, you need a holding space for it. Otherwise, you may eventually forget to remove the item after you've decided to de-own it. Place items in the box yourself and encourage family members to do the same. When the box is full, it's time to donate or sell the items.

DO A DAILY SWEEP

Do a daily sweep or an every other day sweep of your home, prefer-ably before heading to bed. Have family members do their own sweep of their personal areas (like their bedrooms) at the same time. Bring everyone on board to strengthen your new habits of putting things in their places before bedtime. These times are also opportu-nities to clarify routines and responsibilities.

SAY "NO"

Changing the course of your house and your life—in this case, adopt-ing a minimalist lifestyle—can at first require extra time and energy. Save your time and energy for people and activities you love. Say "no, thank you" to a few more activities on your calendar in order to avoid over-scheduling and over-consuming.

DON'T STOCK UP

Stocking up on necessary items sounds like a good idea, right? Even a smart idea. But the problem is that the more space we devote to these items, the more they—and everything else—seem to get lost in an over-stuffed house. When we give too much space to our things, we stock our homes full until we don't remember just what we have.

RENT OR BORROW

If you can't borrow what you need from your friends (whether tools, baby gear, or something else altogether), there's a good chance that somewhere—online or offline—you can find a service that will let you borrow whatever you need for an occasional use. There's no sense in us all buying and storing things we barely use when we can share our belongings with one another.

Long-Term Solutions

Cultivating the habits you've learned so far will help you move from day-to-day to life-long minimalism. They can help you establish a new mindset that propels you along your minimalist path. Here are some additional ways to move your family into minimalism for the long term.

GET RID OF CLUTTER MAGNETS

Define the space you will give your possessions. Get rid of any extra storage containers. If you find a desk or another piece of furniture that keeps attracting clutter, ask yourself if you can do without it. Keep in mind that this particular piece of furniture may not have been a clutter magnet in the past—not until you got rid of the stronger clutter magnets.

SET A LIMIT ON THE NUMBER OF POSSESSIONS YOU CAN HOLD

Minimalism is not about how many possessions you own, but that doesn't mean it's never helpful to count your possessions and keep tabs on that count. I'm not rigid when it comes to counting my things, but there are times when it's helpful to set some loosely-held number boundaries. You decide what the limit is. And you decide if that limit can move up or down. You can count without setting a particular limit, but rather to see a trend more objectively.

INSTITUTE A SHOPPING BAN

Set a period of time where you choose not to buy any non-essentials—a shopping ban. Decide what items are essential (food, toiletries, and so forth) before the ban begins. Invite your partner to join you in the shopping ban. If they aren't interested just yet, start the ban on your own anyway. Show your partner the financial and time benefits of living without things you don't need. If your entire family is on board, note the date on the calendar when the shopping ban is over.

STAY PLUGGED IN

Give yourself encouragement and accountability with the help of a minimalist community. This isn't just about finding support; it's also about finding mutual joy. Many of the experiences we love are much more pleasurable when experienced with other people. Joining an online community and reading minimalist blogs and books will help you enjoy and grow in your own minimalist journey.

RESIST IMPULSE PURCHASES

Corporations and retailers invest billions of dollars to convince us to buy what we really could do without. It takes time, effort, and patience with yourself and your family to learn how to tune out the lies. I like to remind myself that more isn't better, it's just more, and that there's really nothing new under the sun.

STOP BEING BUSY

Minimalism and busyness don't mix well. Tuning out distractions takes time and energy that is better spent elsewhere. If I'm spending nearly all of my time and energy being busy, there's not much left for my friends and family.

SET LONG-TERM MINIMALISM GOALS WITH YOUR FAMILY

Use long-term goals to help keep the clutter out. That could be mean paying off debt with the money you have saved after a six-month shopping ban or taking a family vacation after de-cluttering all your living spaces.

GROW YOUR GRATITUDE

Gratitude changes the way we look at our home, our lives, and the world. Cultivate more gratitude as a way to make minimalism a more permanent part of your life. Gratitude moves you from wanting more to wanting enough. When we focus on what we already have, we can celebrate the present.

Conclusion

We can make sure we stay on our minimalist journey—and keep our family on the journey with us—by implementing these strategies, both big and small. Taken together, they provide us with invaluable tools for both the short and long term.

12 Staying on the Minimalist Path

You've started de-cluttering your house room by room and learned how to maintain your simple spaces. You've gotten your family on board. Once you've done all this, the key to moving forward is to truly enjoy your minimalist home living out your *why*. This is one of the best motivators for both you and your family to live a minimalist lifestyle. Enjoy the time and space you have made for your family to be and stay connected to one another, and to a larger community and purpose.

In addition, always remember what steered you toward minimalism in the first place: your *why*. Also, be sure to consider the stories of minimalists who have gone before you and share your story with others—the ups and the downs. Take time regularly to look at and reflect on your goals and strategies.

Clutter of all kinds will return at times, if only because there are so many ways for it to creep back in! But it will be manageable, and you'll be able to quickly assess the situation and find a solution. You now know which strategies work for you and your family.

I see this as a step-by-step process instead of a quick transformation for those of us who've been steeped in stuff. Remember that your intentional daily habits of removing the inessential will bring you and your family to a lifetime of greater purpose and happiness. I wish you the best in cultivating your minimalist life in your home, in your mind, and in your heart.

Resources

Below you'll find a short list of resources I think you'll find helpful. Many of these books and websites have encouraged me and helped me grow in my journey to live a minimalist lifestyle.

BOOKS

Simplicity Parenting by Kim John Payne

The More of Less by Joshua Becker

Essentialism by Greg McKeown

The Life-Changing Magic of Tidying Up by Marie Kondo

The Joy of Less by Francine Jay

Zero Waste Home by Bea Johnson

WEBSITES

TheMinimalistPlate.com

NoSidebar.com

BecomingMinimalist.com

TheMinimalists.com

TheArtOfSimple.com

MinimalWellness.com

SimpleFamilies.com

ZenHabits.com

BecomingUnBusy.com

BeMoreWithLess.com

SimplifyAndPursue.com

SimpleAndSoul.com

ALifeInProgress.ca

BreakTheTwitch.com

SmallishBlog.com

NourishingMinimalism.com

MissMinimalist.com

References

CHAPTER 1

Feuer, Jack. "The Clutter Culture." *UCLA Magazine*. July 1, 2012. Accessed July 24, 2017. http://magazine.ucla.edu/features/the-clutter-culture.

The True Cost. Dir. Andrew Morgan. Untold Creative, LLC., 2015. Film.

United States National Library of Medicine National Institutes of Health. "Interactions of Top-Down and Bottom-Up Mechanisms in Human Visual Cortex." Accessed July 24, 2017. https://www.ncbi.nlm.nih.gov /pubmed/21228167.

CHAPTER 2

Kim, Zoë. "The Thankful Thread Challenge" *The Minimalist Plate*. Accessed July 24, 2017. http://www.theminimalistplate.com/thankful-challenge.

Mollison, James. "Where Children Sleep" November 2010. Accessed July 24, 2017. http://jamesmollison.com/books/where-children-sleep.

CHAPTER 3

Electronics TakeBack Coalition. "Recycle It Right: Guide to Recycling Your Electronics." Accessed July 24, 2017. http://www.electronicstakeback.com /how-to-recycle-electronics.

Ginsburg, Kenneth R. "The Importance of Play in Promoting Healthy Child Development and Maintaining Strong Parent-Child Bonds." *Pediatrics* 119, no. 1 (January 2007). doi: 10.1542/peds.2006-2697.

"How to Get Personal Data off Your Devices." *Consumer Reports*. February, 2015. Accessed July 24, 2017. http://www.consumerreports.org /cro/2013/11/remove-personal-data-from-any-device/index.htm.

"An Interview with Dr. Stuart Brown, MD." *Publishers Weekly*. Accessed July 24, 2017. http://www.catalystranchmeetings.com/Thinking-Docs /Play-How_It_Shapes_the_Brain.pdf.

CHAPTER 6

Becker, Joshua. "Get Uncluttered in 2017." *Becoming Minimalist*. January 1, 2017. Accessed July 24, 2017. https://www.becomingminimalist.com /get-uncluttered-in-2017.

CHAPTER 7

Becker, Joshua. "Spring/Summer Wardrobe Experiment Recap." *Becoming Minimalist*. January 5, 2010. Accessed July 24, 2017. https://www .becomingminimalist.com/springsummer-wardrobe-experiment-recap.

Gillet, Tracy. "A Rallying Cry to End the Overwhelm of Toys." *Raised Good*. June 12, 2017. Accessed July 24, 2017. http://raisedgood.com /toys-children-less-play.

Payne, Kim John, and Lisa M. Ross. *Simplicity Parenting: Using the Extraordinary Power of Less to Raise Calmer, Happier, and More Secure Kids*. Amazon Digital Services, Inc., 2010. Kindle Edition.

CHAPTER 8

Johnson, Bea. *Zero Waste Home*. Accessed July 24, 2017. http://www.zerowastehome.com.

Walker, Mandy. "How Long to Keep Tax Records and Other Documents." *Consumer Reports*. March 21 2016. Accessed July 24, 2017. http://www .consumerreports.org/taxes/how-long-to-keep-tax-documents.

IRS.gov. "How Long Should I Keep Records?" January 24, 2017. Accessed
      July 24, 2017. https://www.irs.gov/businesses/small-businesses-self
      -employed/how-long-should-i-keep-records.

CHAPTER 10

MacVean, Mary. "For Many People, Gathering Possessions is Just the Stuff
      of Life." *Los Angeles Times.* March 21, 2014. Accessed July 24, 2017.
      http://articles.latimes.com/2014/mar/21/health/la-he-keeping
      -stuff-20140322.

Index

Acknowledgments

I am deeply thankful to my family and friends for all their support and encouragement in writing this book. And a special thanks to my mother, who has been a pillar of wisdom, faith, and encouragement in my life.

I would like to share my appreciation for the many people who had a hand in supporting and bringing this book to life. Thank you to my wonderful editor Susan Randol for guiding me, my publisher Callisto Media, and the many others who poured their time into this book.

I am grateful to the minimalist and intentional living bloggers who have shared my voice on their platforms—especially Robin Shliakhau at *Simplify & Pursue*, Joshua Becker at *Becoming Minimalist*, and Brian Gardner at *No Sidebar*—who mentored me and invested their time in me while seeking nothing in return.

A special thanks to the Hope Writers community, Melissa Camara Wilkins, Krista O'Reilly Davi-Digui, Lisa Avellàn, and Tracey Beers for demonstrating what it means to show up and be vulnerable writing online.

Lastly, I send appreciation and gratitude to my beautiful readers and Facebook community. Without your desire to live better, ask questions, and share inspiration, this book would not exist.

About the Author

Zoë Kim is the founder of *The Minimalist Plate*, a website that inspires families to own fewer possessions to make room for what matters most. She is also a contributor at *HuffPost* and *No Sidebar*.

She's a regular mom of four who found herself stressed and exhausted, spending more time doing things with her stuff than doing things with her family. It was in that stress and exhaustion that her desire to live lighter was born. As she shed her layers of possessions she began to see the real cost of her stuff—and it was way overpriced!

She is passionate about helping other families let go of what's weighing them down so they can find and experience the freedom in owning less.

She lives outside Atlanta with her family.

CPSIA information can be obtained
at www.ICGtesting.com
Printed in the USA
LVHW02s0926131217
559379LV00004B/4/P